54
10/03 2 —N

PRAISE FOR THE KING OF HALLOWEEN
AND MISS FIRECRACKER QUEEN

"With an abundance of wit and memorable detail, Lori Leachman's memoir explores growing up in a household ruled by football, the pros and cons of this sport as controversial on the domestic front as on the field; ultimately, it is the story of her parents' marriage, growing up in the South and then losing the father who stood at the center of it all."

Jill McCorkle author of *Life After Life*, *Going Away Shoes*, *Ferris Beach*, and *The Cheer Leader* among others. Member of the Fellowship of Southern Writers.

"With humor and grace Leachman has woven a tale about a smart, headstrong Southern girl coming of age in a male-centric world. Full of tragedies and triumphs, it is a powerful love story of one family's devotion to a game and to each other."

Katharine Ashe, USA Today bestselling author of *THE DUKE*.

"A daughter's heartwarming account of growing up in a football family. A family's heartbreaking account of dealing with neurodegenerative disease."

Kevin Guskiewicz, MacArthur Genius Award Winner; member NCAA Concussion Committee, NFL Player Mackey-White Association Committee, NFL Head, Neck, and Spine Committee; co-director Matthew Gfeller Sports-Related Traumatic Brain Injury Research Center; director C——— f—— Study of Retired Athletes.

D1402036

"My father, Ken Stabler, suffered from CTE. We saw the symptoms increasing rapidly as he tried diligently to hide them from those closest to him. Fortunately, if that seems even right to say, cancer took his life five months after being discovered. We did see signs of what was to come and, undoubtedly, the CTE would have progressed to the point of robbing him of his mind. Reading Dr. Leachman's book was in a way comforting, knowing that we weren't alone in dealing with this tragic disease. Dr. Leachman gives an authentic voice and story of what it means to live the football life told from a daughter's perspective. Leachman has captured the highs and lows of a life built around competitive sports. With humor and heart she has also presented a convincing, original account of one family's experience with Chronic Traumatic Encephalopathy (CTE)."

Kendra Stabler Moyes personal representative
for Ken Stabler Estates

"I cried. And I laughed. And I cried some more. While Leachman's story of her family's odyssey through the ranks of competitive football, her determination to be true to herself, and one man's struggle with CTE, couldn't be more different from my own, at it's core is a struggle we can all relate to. This book is about family. Identity. Struggle. Finding your voice. And making your way. Bravo for her bravery!"

Jennifer Schlosberg author of
Ill Equipped for a Life of Sex: A Memoir.

"Having played organized football for over twenty years, twelve of those at the highest level, I was blessed to be coached by some of the finest coaches in the world. Lamar Leachman was no doubt the best of the best! His ability to break down film and have his players ready for battle on Sundays was Jedi like. His ability to pay attention to detail and know what the opposition was doing on each play was supernatural. He prepared each day for practice as though it was game day, and on each game day his adrenaline was so high, it was as though he himself was playing the game! His personality was contagious! He lived by a code and prepared each of us by that code—Belief, Effort and Toughness always wins the battle!!! There is no doubt they broke the mold with Lamar Leachman. The story told here will give you a sense of what made him special. I am just grateful I was blessed to be one of the fortunate ones who were able to experience his spirit and enthusiasm before his journey came to an end. Coach, you are missed!"

Marc Spindler, Detroit Lions defensive tackle/end. 1990–1999

the KING *of* HALLOWEEN & MISS FIRECRACKER QUEEN

A Daughter's Tale of Family and Football

Lori Leachman

NEW YORK

LONDON • NASHVILLE • MELBOURNE • VANCOUVER

The King of Halloween and Miss Firecracker Queen
A Daughter's Tale of Family and Football

© 2018 Lori Leachman

All rights reserved. No portion of this book may be reproduced, stored in a retrieval system, or transmitted in any form or by any means—electronic, mechanical, photocopy, recording, scanning, or other—except for brief quotations in critical reviews or articles, without the prior written permission of the publisher.

Published in New York, New York, by Morgan James Publishing. Morgan James is a trademark of Morgan James, LLC. www.MorganJamesPublishing.com

The Morgan James Speakers Group can bring authors to your live event. For more information or to book an event visit The Morgan James Speakers Group at www.TheMorganJamesSpeakersGroup.com.

ISBN 9781614488255 paperback
ISBN 9781683503170 eBook
Library of Congress Control Number: 2017912118

Cover Design by:
Rachel Lopez
www.r2cdesign.com

Interior Design by:
Chris Treccani
www.3dogcreative.net

In an effort to support local communities, raise awareness and funds, Morgan James Publishing donates a percentage of all book sales for the life of each book to Habitat for Humanity Peninsula and Greater Williamsburg.

Get involved today! Visit
www.MorganJamesBuilds.com

For Zach and Colby so they know their legacy.

*To Peter without whom it would not have been possible,
and who paid the highest price.*

TABLE OF CONTENTS

Foreword   by Phil Simms   *xiii*
Foreword   by Harry Carson   *xv*
Preface   *xix*
Introduction   *The King of Halloween*   *xxi*

Part I   **Spring Training and Draft Season**   **1**
Chapter 1   A Fine Romance   3
Chapter 2   Daddy   11
Chapter 3   Momma   19
Chapter 4   Sisters   27
Chapter 5   Southern (Dis)Comforts   37

Part II   **Training Camp or Pre-season**   **51**
Chapter 6   Moving Up and Out   53
Chapter 7   Rambling Wrecks from Georgia Tech;   73
                and then there were three
Chapter 8   Tigers and Gamecocks   91
Chapter 9   Crossing the Mason-Dixon Line   105

Part III   **The Playing Season**   **113**
Chapter 10   Crossing the Border   115
Chapter 11   A Giant Leap   133

Chapter 12   Motor City   149

Part IV: **The Off Season, the Recruiting Season,**
                the Season of the Combines   **155**
Chapter 13   Return Migration   157
Chapter 14   Too Many Hits to the Head   169
Chapter 15   The Price for the Life   177
Chapter 16   The King of Halloween   187

Conclusion   *Miss Firecracker Queen*   *195*
About the Author   *197*
CTE Related Resources   *199*

FOREWORD

By Phil Simms

quarterback New York Giants 1979–1993; Super Bowl XXI most valuable player; analyst CBS's *NFL Today Show*; host *Inside the NFL*.

From 1979 to 1993, I quarterbacked the New York Giants. During my tenure with the Giants we won two Super Bowls based on the strength of both our offense and defense, and the quality of our coaching staff.

During the majority of my time playing for the Giants, Lamar Leachman coached the defensive line. We had a very good relationship. We were always talking about football and our families. There is no doubt we both had a lot in common. I grew up in Kentucky. He grew up in Georgia. We both had similar upbringings, and a tremendous love for football and the NFL.

Lamar was a big personality. He walked around with a lot of swagger. You always knew when he would walk into a room because he was loud; talking and laughing, in a way that always created energy for the team. He had good relationships with everybody. Even though he was a coach and ranked above the players, he could talk their language, laugh with them, and still coach his guys very hard.

The King of Halloween and Miss Firecracker Queen is a tribute to Lamar's spirit as well as a tribute to the football life. It tells the story of one family's rise through the ranks of competitive football, from the unique perspective of a daughter. It also chronicles the Leachman family's struggle to understand and cope with Chronic Traumatic Encephalopathy, the tragic consequence of living such a life.

Reading this book will make you laugh and make you cry. It will make you wish you had grown up in such a family, and make you think twice about a life in football.

FOREWORD

By Harry Carson

inside linebacker New York Giants 1976–1987; member Pro Football
Hall of Fame since 2006; author of *Point of Attack* and *Captain for Life.*

As a player in the National Football League with the New York
Football Giants 'back in the day' (the 1980s), I had the great
opportunity to interact and play for and with many outstanding
coaches and players; coaches like Pro Football Hall of Fame head coach
Bill Parcells and defensive coordinator and linebacker coach Bill Belichick
who is now the head coach of the Super Bowl Champion New England
Patriots. Players like Hall of Famer Lawrence Taylor, and Super Bowl
XXI's Most Valuable Player Phil Simms, are the names that standout
when faithful Giants fans reminisce about winning Super Bowl XXI and
becoming World Champions for the 1986 football season.

Often lost in the discussion of any team's success are the foot soldiers
who do the 'grunt' or dirty work that most people don't see on the surface,
but without which the team cannot succeed. My tenure with the Giants
started in 1976, so I, for one, consider myself one of the ones that was
there playing through those years when the Giants were mediocre at best.
That experience has given me a unique sense of history and perspective.
Our team's success was based not solely on one or two 'stars;' instead
it was based on those players and coaches who in their own way made
a difference by playing the role they were assigned, to the best of their

ability. Such is the case of Lamar Leachman, our defensive line coach. He helped make our New York Giants defense one of the very best in the National Football League. He was a huge reason for the success of our team. The defensive line is always the first line of defense for every team. Without defensive tackles, nose tackles and defensive ends motivated and coached with the techniques and skills to supply an effective pass rush, and without the toughness to hit and shed blockers to help shut down the opposing team's running game, pressure at the linebacker and secondary levels can often be intense and exploited.

Lamar was not my position coach, but we had to work together in meetings and on the field as we implemented defensive strategies. In my role as the captain and leader of the New York Giants Defense, I could clearly see on and off the practice and playing fields the respect his players had for him. He worked his players hard. He was brutally honest if he needed to chastise his guys because he felt they could play better and harder. As hard as he could sometimes be on his players, he loved and respected them. They loved and respected him back. No one ever took his words or actions as a coach personally. As a team, we all appreciated his ability to get the maximum effort from his players.

One of the keys to being a 'good' to 'great player' in any sport is the ability to be 'coachable;' to take direction and be willing to change some type of flaw to improve one's production or effectiveness. This is important for not only the player, but for the team. We all knew Lamar was a 'taskmaster' who loved to coach young players and make them better on the football field. If you attended the Giants practice during training camp, it would not take you long to spot Lamar. He was the one flexing his muscles, wearing the sleeveless tee shirt, barking his approval or disapproval with his heavy southern drawl. He was hard on his players, but they loved it. They loved it because they knew he made them better players on the field. More importantly, he earned their respect for being a straight shooter and treating his players as if they were his own sons. His contributions might never be known by the average football fan, but all who played for him, and were a member of our team, know the essence of the man, and what he meant to us as a team.

Several years ago, I began the process of reuniting the 1986 Super Bowl Championship Team for our 25th Anniversary. Of the 53 men on the team roster, 51 of the players came back. Of the Giants coaches, eight of the eleven coaches from the staff of Bill Parcells were also present. The one coach who was sorely missed by everyone was Lamar. It was our understanding that Lamar sustained a traumatic brain injury because of a freak accident that took place at his home in South Carolina. Brain trauma is a subject that I think I understand, and have spoken out about. I played thirteen seasons in the National Football League. With my collegiate and high school years included, I've played 21 years of football. Those 21 years of hard hitting physical contact have provided me with insight regarding what many former football players and athletes experience. Participants in contact sports like football, rugby, lacrosse, wrestling, boxing, and even NASCAR racing, all worry about cognitive and neurological issues years down the road.

Unfortunately, the neurological issues Lamar Leachman experienced are what many of my former coaches from high school, college, and professional football have also dealt with as they aged. The story told here could just as easily have been their story, behind the scene and after the cheering stops.

PREFACE

I t is amazing how revealing and enlightening funeral celebrations can be. Long-held secrets may finally be shared. The truth of a particular situation is told. Long-simmering resentments are aired, or forgotten. Memories are resurrected. The nature of love is revealed.

I experienced all of these things at my father's funeral in 2012. These revelations brought new context to my entire life. The story told here is my effort to integrate my experiences, and those of my family, with the information that was shared during our mourning of my father's passing, and our celebration of his life and spirit.

This book would not have been possible without Jill Mc Corkle and Ariel Dorfman who charged me with writing my story. Equal thanks goes to Marjorie Hudson, my editor and coach. Without the suggestions and feedback from Katharine Du Bois, I would never have been able to frame the story in such an engaging way. I am indebted to Belle Faber for her discerning mind and eyes. I owe a great debt to my early readers for their comments and feedback: Stephanie Lerner, John Burness, Peter Guzzardi, Doug Zinn, Lisa Barrett, Phil Costanzo, Karen McNamara, Kay Pinto, Anne Bagnal, Kevin Guskiewicz, Anne Lee, David Ferriero, Tina Megaro, Taylor Field Abrams, and Peter Lange. Input from Phil Simms, Bill Kittredge, and Pete Jenkins was essential in helping me more fully frame my father, and his relationships with his players. Emma Smith complied the list of CTE resources. My mother Paula provided constant support and input regarding the realities of each move, as well as their motivations. Andy Farber has lightened my load in ways seen and unseen.

Julienne Alexander and the Morgan James Team brought thier creative juices to bear on the cover. Thank you to Chris Collins and Jeannine Shao Collins for their early interest.

I am also grateful to Terry Whalin, my acquisitions editor. He saw the potential in my story right away. Tiffany Gibson has been instrumental in guiding me through the publishing process. Morgan James Publishing has provided me with a platform to publish my story; for this I am truly grateful and humbled.

The King of Halloween

My daddy was the second child born into a family of four children with an alcoholic father, and born-again Christian mother. He tested the limits of his mother's Christian tolerance with youthful pranks, adolescent drinking, card playing and betting. Grandma Leachman responded with the philosophy of spare the rod, spoil the child. In fairness to her, this was probably an attempt to bring some order to her brood of wild boys, wilder husband, and one darling girl. Nonetheless, her philosophy involved such punishments as locking her children in a black closet when they misbehaved. In theory, they would come to Jesus in the dark, and repent their sins.

For the rest of his life my father could not stand to be in a dark room or darkened space. Upon entering a room or house, his first motion was always to switch on the light. If, on a rare occasion, we would come home and find Daddy home alone, he would have a light on in every room of the house. No doubt this upbringing contributed to the fact that none of the Leachman boys were resilient—except Lamar. And his resilience depended on my mother Paula, his wife. But Paula was no angel. She was the fire in the belly of their collective ambition. She was the fire licking at the heels of my dad's devilishness.

They built a life together on the foundation of competitive football that was both exhilarating and heartbreaking. Football was my family's salvation and destruction. It supported us. It set the pace of our daily lives. It opened doors for us. It provided us with community. Yet, it was the source of our family's greatest sorrow.

This is my story of a football life; a life that was totally male centric, completely focused on physical excellence and mental toughness, never routine, always preoccupied with winning, and continually idolized by those outside of the profession. It was a life characterized by its own particular rhythm and seasons, the seasons of football.

Lamar and Paula on the Blue Ridge Parkway

PART I

Spring Training and Draft Season

Like spring in the traditional calendar, this is the season of new beginnings in football—the season where hope springs eternal. During Spring Training and Draft Season, new players are added, new formations are tried, and personnel may be reassigned to new positions in order to optimize the potential for winning in the Playing Season.

CHAPTER 1

A Fine Romance

"You possess everything to become great."

Native American Proverb

"He who would do great things should not attempt them all alone."

Native American Proverb

"Behind every great man there's a great woman."

American Proverb

The family you think you grew up in is not your real family; it's the family you wanted; the family you hated; the family you love; the family that let you down; the family that lifted you up; the ideal family; the dysfunctional family, your family. The family I grew up in was all of these things, in addition to being middle class, two-parent, white, with two children, until years later, when there were three. While statistically we were more or less average, in reality we knew we were special.

My daddy was a small town country boy with a ticket to the big time called football. My momma was a debutante wanna-be who spent a meaningful part of her formative years in an orphanage and 'foster' homes. They met in the fall of 1955 on the campus of the University of

Tennessee where he was a collegiate football player and she was, as I like to say, Miss Firecracker Queen, voted best body by one fraternity or another; a contest you could only hold in the days before political correctness and fake boobs.

The story of their meeting goes something like this. Momma was with a date at the Fall Football Banquet when she spotted my daddy. She took one look at his handsome face and thick head of brown hair and felt an electric current pulse through her body. She knew they had to meet, so she worked her way into his vision, and then, into his personal space.

"Hello," she said, cocking her head to the side and gracing him with her most coquettish smile. They chatted, and she offered him her number.

Whereupon he asked, in his rich Southern drawl, "Baby, how old are you?"

"Seventeen," she replied.

He stepped back, looked her up and down, and said, "Darlin,' I don't date anybody who's not eighteen. Call me when you grow up."

Since it was the week before Thanksgiving, Momma was not worried. Her birthday was November 27, two weeks away. Thanksgiving break came and went, and with it, her passage into adulthood.

Once back on campus in December, Momma 'arranged' to run into my father. Thus began their whirlwind courtship. Although Daddy had a long-time girlfriend from home Gwen, Momma was not the least bit worried. She knew that she had the goods, and that Gwen did not stand a chance. As she revealed at Daddy's death decades later, she chose him, and that was that.

By the Christmas holiday break, Momma and Daddy were an item. So Momma sent Daddy home with a mission: break up with Gwen. And he did. This act unsettled the entire community. In Cartersville, Georgia, Daddy was the small town boy that made good while Gwen was the daughter of a local lawyer, one of the richest men in town. Dad and Gwen had been the perfect small town, Southern couple; she was rich, and he had talent. They had been going steady for roughly five years, and everyone figured Daddy would marry Gwen right after college. The breakup changed everything. It meant he would not be coming home.

Instead, he married Paula Charlotte (pronounced Shah lot') in a small private ceremony administered by the local Justice of the Peace in Nowheresville, Tennessee. The marriage took place over Easter break, with parents and extended family being informed after the fact. There was no honeymoon. They returned to school, Daddy graduated with a degree in History, and Momma dropped out.

...

Lamar Robert Leachman was the last draft pick in the NFL draft that year. Such a position earns one the title of 'Mr. Irrelevant' in football lore, and so it was for him. He went to Canada to play in the Canadian Football League (CFL) for the princely sum of a few thousand dollars, and Momma went to St. Louis to live with her sister and brother-in-law. By that time, she was obviously pregnant with their first child, my older sister Lisa, and was laying in, as we say in the South, with the only family that would have her.

Daddy played the season in the Calgary cold. When the season was finished he collected his final paycheck of $500 and proceeded to go on a gambling, drinking, and smoking binge that lasted days and left him broke. When he came home to Momma she promptly asked him for his check.

"Well Paula, I cashed that. When I stopped at momma's on the way back I caught up with JR, and Radar, and Howie and the gang, and I lost it all playing cards."

"Lamar you know we have $400 to our names, no jobs, and a baby on the way."

That was the precise moment when Momma took charge of all things financial as well as domestic.

You would have thought that my father would have learned his lesson about card playing, betting and staying out all night, but he was at heart a fun-loving man's man. This got him into plenty of trouble with Momma over the years. When he was coaching high school ball in Savannah, one night he failed to grace the door step at the appointed time. Momma made dinner and eventually put us girls to bed—without Daddy. As the evening drew on, to hear my mother tell it, she just got madder and madder. Once she reached the boiling point, she put on her shoes, checked on us girls, locked the house up, and started the car. She had a pretty good idea of where to find Lamar. Most men, she figured, are creatures of habit and comfort. So she headed down to his local hangout.

Now Momma was a natural beauty, but it did take some effort to carry off her look. Part of that effort involved those big sponge rollers and night cream. By this point in the evening she was creamed and shiny, and rolled up like a big pink bubble head. For modesty's sake she had donned her pink chenille bathrobe and that, along with her sponge rollers and penny loafers, made quite the outfit. But, as she later told me, she did not give a rat's ass what she looked like or who saw her.

As soon as she cruised into the parking lot she spotted Daddy's car. She parked hers, buttoned up that old robe, and strode into the bar with purpose. As she entered, she heard a collective breath from the bar and someone saying, "Would you look at that?" Daddy was not in the main bar, but Momma was not fazed in the least. She knew he was a man who preferred men's company to women's, competition to calm, story-telling to dancing, and card playing to watching TV. By this time she had worked out the fact that card playing and telling lies were what was keeping him out past his due-home time.

She marched into the back room, and sure enough, there was Daddy, at the card table with his buddies. Six men were smoking, sipping whiskey, and fiercely guarding their hands while they slid pennies into the pile at the center of the table. They all looked up simultaneously. Momma did not give them a chance to say a single word before she moved right in on that table and Daddy, saying, "I don't care if you are Jesus Christ and these are your disciples, you had better have your ass home in the next fifteen minutes unless you're lookin' to be crucified." She did not wait for a response nor did she she care if she got one. She turned right around, headed out the way she came in, and drove home. My daddy was home in ten minutes flat.

...

Given Daddy's fun-loving nature, handsome, manly looks and sporty profession, he was a man who men and women wanted to know. Men wanted to impress him while women turned giddy and flirtatious in his presence. On more than one occasion, I heard my dad say something rude and sexist to a woman, and you would have thought he had just told her she was the prettiest, nicest girl in the room. He would say,

"Darlin,' you're quite the honey, aren't you."

"That is one hard body you've got there honey."

"Baby, I could stack that rack."

Such comments would generate a charge of sexual harassment in this day and age. They would surely be considered acts of micro-aggression against woman. But in the 1960s and early 1970s it was still a man's world, and football was the most manly of popular sports. Women hearing Daddy's cracks just swooned harder. Men fell all over themselves to be his buddy. I am sure that this fact is part of the reason that, to this day, I have no patience for women who preen and fawn over men. Nor do I tolerate well celebrity fetishes or jock hounds, regardless of sex, nor does my mother.

My older sister Lisa Lucille was born on January 19, 1957. This date is exactly nine months after my parents where married. While I have my suspicions regarding the actual marriage date and the insistence by my mother of their post marriage sexual consummation, that's her story and she's sticking to it. Be that as it may, one thing that was clear throughout my parent's fifty-plus years of marriage was that they had chemistry. I recall many an afternoon when my parents locked themselves in their bedroom after forcing my sister and me to go out and play.

We did not always obey this command. Many afternoons I could be found sitting, whining and crying by my parents' bedroom door, sweating in the Southern heat and humidity, waiting for them to reemerge. If their session of afternoon delight was especially leisurely, by the time they cracked open their bedroom door, I would be back flat to the floor, knees bent, legs crossed, staring up at the hall ceiling. I would be sucking my thumb, twirling my hair, and pumping my crossed leg to the rhythm of my twirls, engrossed in my own personal twilight zone of comfort and satisfaction.

Chemistry aside, they were like many young couples in the 1950s; Daddy got a job as a high school football coach and history teacher, and Momma assumed the job of mothering. But my mother was smart, socially aware, and driven in a 1950's kind of way. She understood the striations of social class, and the characteristics necessary to move up. She did not possess personal ambition, but she was fiercely ambitious for her mate and her children. For that purpose, she knew that it was imperative that she go back to school and finish her degree.

She also knew that my dad had the capabilities to be really successful in his chosen field. She understood that he was a wild stallion; fierce, willful, reckless, beautiful, and strong. All of that energy needed to be channeled into productive directions if he was going to amount to much, for he was also a guy who loved to party. My mother's mission, and her compromise for the rest of her life, was to help him achieve his potential.

From the first days of their marriage my mother tutored my father. Among other things, she helped him overcome a serious stutter, since she knew it would be an impediment to his moving up the coaching ranks. Throughout Daddy's childhood, every Sunday the Leachman brood was cleaned up and marched into the First Baptist Church. The typical Sunday religious experience involved raising one's hands in praise for the Lord, and being cold-called for scripture recital from the pastor in his pulpit. In front of the entire congregation, my daddy rarely missed a hallelujah or scripture quote, but he sure did develop a furious and persistent stutter.

Some of my earliest childhood memories are of my daddy laid back in his cheap vinyl recliner—we could not afford the likes of a La-Z-Boy at that time. He would be doing the vocabulary test from the *Reader's Digest* while Momma cooked dinner. As the the meal was simmering, Daddy would pronounce the words, modulate his breath and stand corrected—or not—by Momma. My mother was such a good partner and teacher and, my daddy such a motivated student, that by the time he was thirty he had overcome that stutter. As his career progressed, he was often solicited for public speaking engagements, both paid and unpaid.

Daddy knew how to coach but had no idea how to teach. Momma knew she could help with that too. His needs and her ambitions led her to enroll in a teacher's college in the fall of 1957. Within a few years she had an education degree and a job teaching sixth grade in the school my sister and I would eventually attend. She gave birth to me during the spring of 1958 without missing a beat or a term.

Having been inculcated with the fear of God early on, Daddy was fiercely committed to Lisa's and my salvation. He did not care one whit where we went to church or which youth group we joined, as long as it was nominally Christian, only that we did so. The consequence of this approach was that over the years, Lisa and I attended the Baptist Church, the Presbyterian Church, the Methodist Church, the Catholic Church, the Non-denominational Church—today it would most likely be Unitarian—the Church of Fear and Righteousness, and the Church of Joy and Grace. It was a heady mix that left me with an openness to all religions, a belief in none in particular, and a healthy scorn for The Church.

Over the years, the effects of all of Daddy's early childhood religious indoctrination dissipated. By the time Lamara, my younger sister, was in school and Lisa and I were in college, attending church regularly and participating in a youth group were no longer mandatory. However, Daddy always had his eye on salvation and the devil. This probably had something to do with the fact that he had a good bit of devilishness in him, knew his fair share of temptation, and had been brought up to crave salvation.

CHAPTER 2

Daddy

"Great souls have wills; feeble ones have wishes."

Chinese proverb.

"A man who cannot tolerate small ills can never accomplish great things."

American proverb.

"The most reliable way to predict the future is to create it."

Abraham Lincoln

Lamar Robert Leachman was born in the back bedroom of a shotgun house in 1932 in small-town Georgia. His father worked as a mechanic at a gas station owned by one of his brothers. Since Grandpa Leachman was one of eleven children, there were many Leachman boys and kin spread throughout this rural Georgia region. The Leachman network provided my grandfather with plenty of drinking buddies and distractions, since Grandpa was known to work hard and play hard in the days before this was a youthful slogan. He smoked two packs of Pall Malls a day and counted on his wife Eula Susie Mae to keep him right with God. Such a task was right up Eula's alley, since she was known to 'fall out with the Lord,' as they say, and speak in tongues during the many revivals that passed through the rural South.

From an early age, Daddy knew that sports were his love and his ticket to a bigger life. As the middle child of three boys—his sister Eva being a girl did not even register on his radar—he practiced physicality early and often. By high school it was clear that Daddy had the gift for football. He was such a talented player that in those days he played both offense and defense. This fact clearly contributed to the eight youthful concussions he recalled having. Despite those injuries, his accomplishments on the Cartersville Hurricanes athletic field were legendary. He won many awards, both social and athletic. In fact, in the early 1950s Lamar set the Georgia High School Football Rushing Record. He held that record until it was finally broken by Herschel Walker in 1979. For those of you who are not football aficionados, Walker went on to win the Heisman Trophy as a star player for the University of Georgia. For his efforts, Daddy was recruited by General Robert Neyland to join the Volunteers, receiving a football scholarship to the University of Tennessee (UT).

He spent five years at the University of Tennessee playing with Johnny Majors, Doug Atkins, and numerous other football greats. He and his teammates played in the 1952 Cotton Bowl. Here again, his talent was such that he played both offense—as #10, center—and defense—as #55, linebacker. During his freshman year at UT he was red-shirted, and at some point in his college career he hurt his knees, resulting in the five-year college plan, the last place in the 1955 NFL draft, and the serendipity of meeting my mother in her freshman year.

...

Once he cut his ties to Gwen, Daddy never appeared to want to go back to Cartersville. But for a brief time in 1967, our family had to live there. We were moving from Richmond, Virginia, to Atlanta, Georgia, so that Daddy could take a coaching job at Georgia Tech. For the first two months of that move, Momma, Lisa, and I lived with Grandma and

Grandpa Leachman in their little house off of the Access Road—that was indeed its name—of Interstate 75. Daddy, however, stayed at the office and came up only on the weekends. Lisa and I slept heel to head on a brick-hard fold-out couch in the living room while my mother, and father on the weekends, slept in the spare bedroom. We all sweated through the night listening to the trucks whoosh by, while Lisa and I had the added burden of trying not to touch each other.

After one particularly sleepless night when Lisa and I tortured each other with touch and sweat, and each effort to descend into sleep was interrupted by the sound and vibrations from passing trucks, I said to Grandma Leachman, "The noise from the road is so bad we can't sleep." My grandmother replied, "I love the traffic. It soothes me." We knew there was nothing to be done about our predicament.

For those two months we had the eye-opening experience of attending Cartersville Elementary School. The school was a two-story wooden structure with no air conditioning, and a collective psychology that reflected the racial prejudices of the 1950's South. Given that the school was close to fifty percent black, the presence of such a mindset was somewhat confounding to Lisa and me, yet somehow consistent with the broader community sentiment of Cartersville.

One Saturday Lisa and I went to the local movie theatre. As we entered we confronted a sign that read "Blacks Only" in large white lettering. It directed the African American patrons up to the balcony, the hottest place in the theatre, of course. At the local public swimming pool black kids hung on the fence gazing longingly at the water, since the pool was open only to whites. When we asked our mates at the pool why none of the blacks kids were allowed in they responded, "Would you want to swim with a nigger?" We did not understand the weight of the issue nor the level of ignorance that fostered such sentiments. In our football world, blacks had always been present, because they were generally good at sports. Since competition was king, it trumped race. We were shocked by Cartersville and, like Daddy, could not get out of there fast enough.

Yet, we did return often, especially during our years living in Atlanta. This had something to do with the fact that Daddy was a bit of a local celebrity. Our typical visits would be for the weekend where we would spend the day swimming at the private pool at the Elk's Lodge, and Momma and Daddy would go out at night leaving us with Grandma and Grandpa Leachman. Lisa and I loved that pool at the Elk's Lodge, for it was always filled with kids large and small, and had a low and high diving board.

For many years both Momma and Daddy worked at a local pool in the summers, because we needed the money. My dad was the head lifeguard, and my mother worked the snack bar. So both Lisa and I could swim from an early age—Daddy 'taught' us using his shock approach. When I was about the age of three my father offered me some simple instruction and threw me in the pool. "Kick Lori, kick. Here to the side. I'll pull you out." It was frightening—a sink or swim moment. I produced my best dog paddle and kicked my legs with a vengeance. As I approached the side, my dad plucked me from the water and plopped me down on the concrete. We repeated this exercise, accompanying it with some more instruction regarding body positioning and how to more effectively use my arms, "Try to stroke through the water like this, not slap it. Make a cup of your hands to push the water away." Eventually, I felt confident jumping off the diving board and working my way to the ladder in the deep end. Only after I had mastered this trick did I graduate to formal lessons, and cultivate grace and fluidity in the water.

One particular Sunday when we were living in Atlanta and Lisa and I were about eleven and ten, Lisa and I, along with around ten other kids, lined up for the Elk's Lodge high dive. We started with diving and cannon balls until, at some point, one kid or another upped the ante to flips. At first that was a real no-go for me as flips were a new maneuver. But never underestimate the power of youthful peer pressure and sibling competition—Lisa nailed it on the first run—combined with your daddy's goading. Up I went walking slowly to the end of the board—nothing looks higher than when you are looking down from it. I was petrified, but all the kids were yelling, and whistling, and splashing for me to, "Just go already!" So I took the leap, tucked, and twirled. Splat! Right on my back, a hard landing in the water. My buddies collectively sucked in their breath. From the side Daddy yelled, "Get up and try it again."

Now that was the last thing I wanted to do. But, when you are a called out in front of your group, and bested by your sister, you have no other option if you want to save face. So I repeated the exercise to the same result. Again my father told me to try it again, offering some small instruction on the tuck move. "Tighten up your grip. Hug your legs to your chest. Like this," he said, as he pulled his knees up against his chest and firmly crossed and grasped his muscular forearms across them. Again, splat on my back.

By now the whole pool was watching. Kids and adults were clinging to the sides or doggie paddling in place. Those in the shallow end were simply standing still, all faces upturned expectantly to the high dive. After two more tries my back was on fire as though a whole colony of red ants were feasting on me. I was blubbering, and trying hard to suck the snot back into my nose. My dad was saying that I had to keep trying until I got it right, for that was his creed. This is the point where Paula enters the picture—she was always the voice of reason and restraint in the family—and interceded on my behalf.

"Lamar, that's enough," she said, as she place her hand in a gentle, but firm way on his broad shoulder, and leaned into his ear. "She gave it a good try. She can try it again another day, on the low board first."

Daddy, looking up at her, nodded his assent. Then he pierced me with his stare, and turned away. Although I knew I had failed in some insignificant, yet important way, I was overcome with relief. I have never forgotten that humiliation, nor the disappointment in my father's eyes.

What is most interesting about this story is that after I wrote it down, and asked my sister Lisa to read it, she told me she thought that she was the one who couldn't master the flip. The more I have thought about that, the less certain I have become about who exactly was confronting failure on the high dive. But what is most fascinating about it is that we both recall it the same way, and we both took on board the lesson of failure and Daddy's disappointment from the episode, even if that failure belonged to the other.

...

On these weekend visits to Cartersville, if the season was such that the Elk's Lodge pool was closed or the weather uncooperative, Grandpa Leachman would take us girls out for coconut cream pie, and then to the strip mall. He would give us each a dollar for the Walgreens. He never came in with us; he just sat in the car with the window rolled down, his arm hanging out, smoking. He was engaging in what he called 'eyeballing'— watching the world go by, staring at things and people—and, as we later would learn, not infrequently indulging in a nip or two from his flask.

One day Grandpa took us to the strip mall and dropped us off in front of the Walgreens. He then parked the car, rolled down his window, lit a cigarette, and commenced his eyeballing and waiting. Lisa and I slipped into the store and eventually meandered to the record section. We both decided to use our wealth to buy our first albums. I still remember mine, it was *Diana Ross and the Supremes Join the Temptations*. When I brought that record back to the car and showed Grandpa Leachman all he could say was, "Why do you want to listen to nigger music?" I had no idea how to answer that. Change came very slowly to residents of Cartersville, and for most of the elderly, it never came at all.

Just like prejudice, alcohol was a thing my Grandpa had trouble overcoming. Sometimes when we visited Cartersville, Grandpa wasn't there. When we asked where he was we would be told that he was 'on vacation' or, 'in the hospital.' As young children we had no idea what either of those meant, or even if they were materially different, after all we had never been to a hospital. But one thing we did know was that Grandpa loved to eyeball, and, he could even do it sitting in his driveway looking at the fence that separated his house from the bank and the Access Road. Our company simply provided him a cover.

I used to go out there and sit with him. We would perch ourselves on the running board of his old black Ford. It was one of the 1940s versions of the Ford Coupe, with bulbous wheel wells connected by a running board on either side. He would smoke Pall Malls, we would eyeball the fence, and every once in a while he would reach back under the front seat. He would draw out a silver flask, or in particularly indulgent periods, a fifth of vodka? gin? moonshine? something clear—and take a nip. The conversation was sparse, but the camaraderie we had was real and heartfelt.

"Lori, did you know that this car belonged to my brother Charlie first? He was my half brother. Ten years younger. Dead. Died in the war. He's buried in the Leachman family cemetery."

"We have a family cemetery? Where?"

"Way up country in the holler near Canton. I'll take you there some day."

And he did. And I was shocked, and a bit afraid—the houses were shacks on stilts with raw, unpainted wood exteriors. Did they have running water? electricity? I had no idea because I stuck close to the car and refused to climb the rickety open steps leading to the porches.

If it was raining outside we would sit in lawn chairs under the tar-papered roof of the garage. Grandpa Leachman would tuck his cigarettes into his breast pocket and his flask into the large side pocket of his navy blue coveralls, drawing from each pocket at regular intervals. The driveway and the detached garage, I realized years later, were his drinking spots, since Eula was a woman of God who would not allow alcohol in her home.

CHAPTER 3

Momma

"I hope that I may always desire more than I can accomplish."
Michaelangelo

"You cannot fail unless you quit."
Abraham Lincoln

"A man wrapped up in himself makes a very small package."
Ben Franklin

Paula Charlotte Davis was born in Detroit, Michigan in 1937 to the daughter of the Lafayette County, Tennessee School Superintendent and local farmer, and to a welder with a large family, and an even larger temper. I knew her dad as PaDavis. MaMa (pronounced Ma' mah), as we called Momma's mother, married PaDavis young to escape her own father's neglect and her stepmother's wrath. When she was sixteen they moved to Detroit where PaDavis took a union job in the auto industry, and MaMa finished high school. She got a job as a saleswoman at a local department store. Shortly thereafter she produced two daughters in quick succession. One day when Momma was approaching seven and Aunt Patty, her sister, nine, MaMa packed the girls in the car while PaDavis was at work and headed back to Tennessee. She had had enough of being broke, beaten, and abused, and was sure that life was better back where she came from.

Jobs were scarce in rural Tennessee in the early 1940s, so MaMa enrolled in nursing school. In time she found that she simply could not handle the demands of school, work, and children. So she dropped out. She took a job as a sales girl at Harvey's, a family-owned department store chain in Tennessee. There was no daycare system for young children in the 1940s, nor were there after-school programs. As a consequence, MaMa was forced to place her girls in an orphanage, and then with a series of foster families. For years Paula and her older sister Patty lived close by with a number of different families. MaMa visited the girls on holidays and Saturdays. But, the girls spent their summers and the bulk of their holiday vacations with a series of aunts and uncles from PaDavis' side.

For Paula and Patty, this was a difficult and unstable period. During the school term, they lived together with at least two different families in twice as many years. In the summers they would be separated, with Paula going to live with Aunt Mabel and Uncle Ray, who were eventually joined by Aunt Lura after she was widowed. Patty, on the other hand, was housed with Aunt Sister and Uncle Doc. As Patty recalls it, Paula got the good, stylish aunt, while she was placed with the frumpy and more conventional Davis sister.

As young girls, my sister Lisa and I would regularly visit these aunts and uncles. Typically mom would drive us there; dad rarely came along. We would leave early in the morning and arrive in the late afternoon. Momma would lead us in spelling games from signs along the highway to pass the time.

"Girls, you see that sign to Ruby Falls? Spell four words that start with r and end in y."

"R-a-i-n-y, like a rainy day," said Lisa.

"R-a-y, like a ray of sunshine." I said. I was the worst speller, still am.

Sometimes we would stop in Cartersville to break up the trip. Lisa and I would sleep on that brick hard sofa, sweating through the night, fighting over space. We would continue our battles in the car the next day if we both ended up in the back seat together. The heat in both domains was relentless. It built up during the day in the car like a blast furnace. Your legs would stick to the hot plastic seats as the wind whipped your hair around your face. The damp, still nighttime air acted like an insulating blanket. The lack of relief simply reinforced our agitation with one another. By the time we arrived, we were always worse for the wear.

On one such trip we broke up the drive by stopping at a roadside strip of stores for snacks. To grab a bit of air conditioning, we wandered into a small strip mall clothing store. On one of the tables—no racks or hangers here, which will tell you something about the class of the merchandise—I came across a blue and white polka dot bikini with a detachable skirt. Well, that was a number I simply had to have. I begged and begged, and wore Momma down. Since I was fat as a sausage with those rolls in the thighs that are cute on babies but no one else, it was not an optimal fashion selection. That did not stop me from loving that bikini, wearing it every chance I got, and fretting over whether to go with, or without the skirt on this or that particular day.

Once we arrived at our Tennessee destination and collected ourselves, we would commence the visiting. Lisa and I would play tag and hide and seek in the local dry goods store owned by Uncle Ray and Aunt Mabel, while Momma, Ray, and Mabel would catch up over a glass of icy cold, sweet tea. The store was one of those old brick buildings with large, street-facing windows. It had an open second floor for inventory and office space, and wide aisles with moveable shelving and display tables. Every time we visited we found the layout somewhat changed, making it a novel playground. We played dress up at the large vanity in Aunt Lura's bedroom, using her silky slips as our ball gowns. After all, she was one of the more stylish aunts. We loved the three-quarter mirror in the center for it afforded us a full body view of our chosen getup. The side mirrors enabled us to check out our rear view, a thing we could not do with ease at home. We stopped by Uncle Harold's dry cleaners for a visit. And, we saw pictures and heard stories about Uncle Doc and Aunt Sister, never having a clear sense of who they were, or how they were related to us. In fact, we did not fully understand their places in our lives until after my father died, when some small pieces of my mother's story began to emerge.

Uncle Doc was the local town physician and Aunt Sister was his drug addicted wife—laudanum, I presume. Aunt Sister, having raised PaDavis and his siblings, Harold, Mabel, and Lura among them, never had children of her own. For Doc and Aunt Sister, Momma and Aunt Patty served as proxies.

When my older sister Lisa was dating the person who would become her second husband, she invited me to dinner one night to meet some of his family. When I asked who would be there she said, "Brother." I responded, "I know Jon's brother will be there, but what's his name?" Lisa said again, "Brother." At that point I broke out laughing and told her she had to be kidding; what grown man is called Brother? That led us to a discussion about how Southern Jon's family must be. You see, at that time I had totally forgotten that we had an Aunt Sister. It was only years later, looking at old photos, that I recalled our own family nomenclature.

...

My mother and her sister lived the nomadic life for almost four years. During that time, MaMa, being smart as a whip, and driven by neglect and poverty, divorced Pa Davis and worked her way up through the Harvey's hierarchy. She became a buyer and then merchandise manager of soft goods for the entire Harvey's chain. She worked for the company for over fifty years. For the last thirty, she was on a first name basis with Mr. Harvey, the store's founder. She traveled to and from New York City regularly, selecting clothing, bedding, and other textile products for the Harvey's chain, and cultivating her refined style.

Something her children never recall seeing simultaneously is MaMa with a smile and a drink. To her children, and to us, her grandchildren, she was always a serious business woman. However, in the 1940s, MaMa vacationed in Cuba. We only know this from a photograph that we discovered after her death. In it she is wearing a stylish dress with a fitted bodice and a full circle skirt. She is sitting on a bar stool surrounded by men. She has a drink in one hand, and a big smile on her face. Clearly, during this period she was a woman about town; catching up on the things she had missed in her youth, and dating a series of dashing men.

In 1946 MaMa was having lunch in the neighborhood diner around the corner from Harvey's flagship downtown store when she was approached by a local postal worker named Raymond Handy. Ray was a thirty-five year old bachelor with a good job, a solid bank account, and honorable intentions. They married three years later.

During the dating-Ray period, MaMa collected Paula and Patty from their foster family and brought them to Nashville to live with her. They were eleven and thirteen by this time. They shared a small apartment on Stratton Avenue in east Nashville. A year or so later MaMa married Ray, and the new family moved into a duplex on 16th Street.

Momma recalls that the adjustment to this new family composition was difficult, especially on Aunt Patty. Raymond was strict, and was clearly not the girls' father. As a result Patty married as soon as she could—at eighteen, to the local high school genius, Alton. They graduated the year that they were married and moved to St. Louis. In St. Louis, Alton attended St. Louis University on a full scholarship. This left Momma at home and the sole focus of attention and discipline. But, as Momma recalls, she was not much of a discipline problem. The first time she stepped out of line MaMa informed her, "Paula, you know there's still a slot at St Mary's Orphanage with your name on it. If you cannot obey the rules, be home on time, and perform up to your potential in school, we can settle you back in tomorrow." So she towed the line, snapped on her strand of pearls, and became a model of well-behaved young womanhood.

About the time that Patty and Alton married, when Momma was sixteen, MaMa produced the first of two sons for the Handy clan. Career woman that she was, she promptly left them to be raised by a series of housekeepers, the most important of whom were Miss Edith and Miss Bessy. Both boys recall their mother coming home from a day at the office and heading straight to the bath. Once Mama was relaxing in the tub, Raymond would bring her her 'regular' of cookies, or crackers, and something to drink. He would perch on the toilet seat while Mama luxuriated in the bath, and they would discuss their day.

"Mother," Ray would say, " did you manage to order the new curtains for the living room? And did you return the call to Dave's teacher?"

"Dad," MaMa would respond, "I have the curtains on order. I left a message for Mrs. Smalls, but was away from my desk for most of the day, so I missed her call. I'll try her again tomorrow. Can you hand me that cloth by the sink?"

And so it went, secure in the steam and relative peace of the bath until it was time to tuck the boys in bed.

In the Handy household, my impression as a young girl was that MaMa was the pragmatic, professional woman, and Grandpa Handy was the nurturer and home body. Grandpa Handy would hold you in his lap and rock you. He would play with you in the fort he built for the boys in their back yard. He would ride you on the riding lawn mower as he manicured their lawn. MaMa, on the other hand was always coming from, or going to, work, smartly dressed and totally groomed. I never once recall her sitting on the floor with her boys, or Lisa and me, engaging in our play.

While I did not understand or support the lack of mothering exhibited by my grandmother, I always admired her sense of style, her sophistication, and her drive. These impressions were reinforced by the fact that MaMa always carried, in the crook of her arm, a designer bag and, in her later years, she wore a Cartier watch on her wrist. At her death she willed me one fine mink. On one of her buying trips she took us to tea at the Algonquin. At the age of sixty, she finally earned her university degree.

At one point, when she was close to eighty, MaMa and I were having a conversation about women and work. "MaMa," I said, "you know you were a woman ahead of your time." She paused, looked at me as she was sorting utensils from the dishwasher, and responded after a moment of thought, "You know, I was. But Lori, I did not have a choice."

It is surely the case that what my mother did not get from her mother in the form of nurturing, she made up for by building on MaMa's sense of style, and her fierce determination. What is also clear after many years, is that my mother's commitment to family above all else—including truth and honesty—is a direct result of her perception that her own mother lacked this. All those years of domestic turbulence simply cemented mother's determination to do it differently.

The other trait Momma got from MaMa was a love of having a nice car. MaMa took great pride in her cars and was driving herself until her death at 92. For many years, MaMa would sell Momma her used Cadillac when she was ready for a new model. For all of her adult life my mother has been a smoker, using a small brown cigarette filter. In her Cadillac car, sporting an open, beautiful smile, long flowing auburn hair—in her later years blonde—and brandishing an endless chain of lit cigarettes, mother knew she cut a glamorous figure behind the wheel.

I remember champagne Cadillacs with white leather seats, beige Cadillacs with beige leather seats, and black Cadillacs with beige leather seats. They had electric windows, fold down arm rests, and air conditioning before those features were the norm. Eventually, Momma switched to MaMa's hand-me-down BMWs because, as MaMa aged, she "felt more comfortable driving a smaller car."

CHAPTER 4

Sisters

"When I let go of what I am, I become what I might be."

Lao Tzu

"What lies in our power to do, lies in our power not to do."

Aristotle

"He who cannot bear the small is not capable of the great."

Irish proverb

Lisa and I were steeped in competition from an early age. Being the younger of two girls born fourteen months apart, I generally ended up on the losing end of the exchange. Nonetheless, competition with Lisa is an elemental piece of who I am. I am the younger sibling, the fat one, the one with carrot red hair and glasses. Needless to say, these characteristics have not always contributed positively to my sense of self-esteem. In our youth, the closeness that we shared could have turned us into an invincible team facing the world; instead, we fought, and I compared.

As young girls, Lisa was always the pretty one. I was always the happy one. My mother once said to me, "Lori, I don't worry about you like I do the others because you have the innate ability to be happy. You are joyful."

At the time I found it rather hurtful, because when you are competing for your parents' attention you want to be at the top of their thoughts, even if it is due to worry. Now that I am older, I know a happy nature is my blessing. Yet, throughout my life this difference between us has meant that I got the least from my parents emotionally.

I was the child who sucked her thumb and wet her bed. For the longest time—thirteen years to be precise—I was also the baby. This meant that Lisa got to do everything before I did, or so it seemed. The only thing that I can recall beating her to is growing breasts. Mine came on early, in fifth grade, and were large and round. One morning as I was sitting at the yellow formica breakfast bar that bisected our kitchen, scooping cereal into my mouth, my dad swept by and popped my bra strap to let me know he had noticed. I almost choked; I was totally embarrassed.

As the child of the Firecracker Queen and the Football Star, breasts could have been a trump card for a confident girl. Instead, they made me uncomfortably self-conscious. That self-consciousness was compounded by the fact that Lisa took it upon herself to make me my first bra. It was made out of beige stretchy material with ribbon for straps. It hooked in the back like a traditional bra although the hooks and eyes were much messier, in part due to the hand sewn nature of the contraption. I was so offended by it, and her actions, that it delayed my willingness to wear a bra for months, a fact that the boys in the neighborhood loved, since they could ogle my bouncing breasts as I ran the bases in the neighborhood kickball game or dribbled the ball in soccer.

In the end, Lisa has even bested me on this dimension. Lisa was extremely flat-chested until she undertook her 'augmentation procedure'—the specific medical term for such enhancements. She now sports a fabulous pair of store-bought knockers that have been known to make grown men sigh. Even she has been surprised by the power of her round bosoms. Upon returning to work with her new breasts after a long Thanksgiving break, she recounted the following incident.

At the time, Lisa was vice president for a Southern manufacturing firm. She was the first woman to hold that position in this firm, where, like

Carly Forina, she had worked her way up from secretary and switchboard operator—and yes, we still had manually operated switch boards in the South in the 1980s. Her current position required that she tour the production facilities regularly to ensure that operations were functioning smoothly. On this particular week in mid-December she donned her hard hat, wearing her typical three inch heels and conservative navy blue dress. It is important to note that this particular dress had a collar right up to the neckline. She proceeded to move through the factory. On the factory floor she began her inspection of each station, asking pertinent questions, and feigning great attention. At each and every stop the men, for only men worked in this factory, complemented her on how robust and well she was looking. They had no specific idea what was different, but she could see that they were sure attentive and aroused in a way that none of them had been before in her presence.

Since my dad was a breast man, he also noticed. The first summer after her procedure, on the first day of our annual family vacation to the beach, my dad pointed out, "Lisa, you know you are now a hard body." I knew I would never earn that designation.

...

While my youthful self-esteem was suspect, my will was strong. From the age of three, I wore glasses to correct my near-blind vision. I loved those glasses and the gift of crisp vision that they provided. But, one day Momma said "no" to a childish request. So I decided to get even. I understood that my glasses were necessary, and expensive. I went into my bedroom, closed the door, and proceeded to take my cat-eyed glasses off of my face. I then laid the lenses down on the floor, got on my hands and knees, and placed my hands over each lens. I brought all of my weight to bear on top of those glasses and scraped them around the edge of the rug until there was a path in the hardwood, and my glasses' lenses looked like a foggy shower door. Then I broke them in two at the nose.

Momma was busy in the kitchen, so I marched in there and presented them to her in the palm of my fat little hand. My mother took one look and busted my butt. She taped my glasses together with medical tape at the nose and made me wear them for weeks, until we could afford a new pair. The only way I could see anything was to push my glasses around so that I could see through the edges of the lenses. I sure showed her.

Even the gentlest of older sisters has been known to exploit her advantage. Lisa quickly became a master at this. When I was four, Lisa, Momma, and I were at the Red and White and I wanted candy. Momma denied this desire, so I decided to sate it myself when she wasn't looking. I stole the object of my attention, a piece of penny candy. My sister saw me and threatened to tell our mother unless I did everything she asked of me. I became a slave to my sister's desires for over a year.

"Lori, I'm gonna tell mom about the candy if you don't let me go first."

"Lori, I want to sit there. Move over, or I'll tell mom."

"Lori, I get the front seat unless you want mom to know about the candy."

Lisa was merciless in her use of this leverage. But, one Saturday I had had a year's worth of simmering resentment, and I finally refused her request to move over in the back seat of the car. She immediately propped her chin on the front seat back and spilled the beans.

"Momma, you know when we were at the Red and White last summer? Well, Lori stole some candy on the way out and ate it."

"Momma, it was only one piece, and Lisa has been making me wait on her ever since," I whined.

My mother laughed until she cried, which made me cry. She said, "Well, I guess you paid for that."

On another Saturday drive, this time with both Momma and Daddy, we cruised around town and to Tybee Beach. For the first part of the drive it was lots of fun with the windows down and music playing on the radio. I have a clear picture of my mom's shoulder-length auburn hair blowing in the wind like a movie star, my dad's strong, muscular arm draped over the front seat back, his left hand on the steering wheel. Intermittently, my mother's scent of Jungle Gardenia would blow through the back seat, creating the sensation of walking past a gardenia bush on a hot, breezy day. As the drive went on, I had to use the bathroom. My dad simply refused to stop or pull over saying, "Lori, you can hold it a while longer."

Finally we arrived at the home of some of his friends. Seems Daddy had a mission all along. However he would not let us girls out of the car. "You girls stay here until I check to see if they're home." I realize now that he must have been checking to see if the coast was clear to bring his family to this bachelor pad. By the time Daddy disappeared into the building I was crying in the back seat—I had to go so badly. Finally, I stood up in the well of the back seat and peed all over the floor.

As Daddy strolled back to the car to collect us my mother said, "Lamar, what took you so long? Lori couldn't hold it any longer. She peed on the floor of the back seat. I've cleaned it up as best I can." There ensued a lengthly discussion about whether to go in, or not, until it was finally settled. We would go in for a short visit. I would simply leave my soiled panties in the car. Since I had on a dress, no one there needed to know what had happened.

The two men we were visiting were dad's coaching buddies. They were big, burly men not unlike my father. The visit progressed in a sociable and pleasant manner until Lisa and I got bored with the game we had made up, and I got the bright idea that I could swing over Daddy's crossed leg. I laid my belly across his calf and took to swinging with gusto. The room exploded into laughter. "Hot damnit, Paula!" my dad bellowed. Turns out every swing was a big beaver shot straight to the heart of those two young men. When I realized the laughing was directed at me, I immediately knew why. I ran and locked myself in the bathroom. I refused to come out until it was time to leave.

Since this incident, I have always had a hang-up about using the bathroom repeatedly before I leave the house. I am also extremely sympathetic to others needing to stop on a road trip, no matter how recent the last stop was. This is something my second husband had no patience for, since for him, every road trip was test of whether you could better your previous time, or, set a new family record for that route and distance.

It never ceases to amaze me how some personality types just need to make a competition out of everything. For example, at one point in our youth Lisa and I were having breakfast one morning at the yellow formica bar when my father came in and asked,

"Lisa, how'd you do on your history test?"

"I got a 93."

"Lori, how 'bout you? How'd you do on your math test?"

"I got an 89."

"Why? What happened? Lisa got a 93 on her test. Surely you're as smart as she is."

I responded, "I don't understand why we have to compete with one another when we have to compete with everyone else out there."

"Because, life's a competition. If you aren't in it to win it, why bother?" Daddy said placing his hands on the bar top, his intense stare pinning me in place with earnest conviction.

A thousand possible responses were rolling around in my mouth, fizzing furiously like that first sip of a carbonated drink: "Because we have to." "Because you said to." "Because it's interesting, but not that…" I clamped my mouth shut. I knew this was not a debate.

...

When we were little, Lisa and I had a big brother of sorts. His name was Bud. He was a cute boy with brown hair and eyes, an open face, and a ready smile. He was one of Daddy's high school players. His father was in the military and was being transferred to Florida in Bud's senior year. Bud was a talented player and had the prospect of earning a football scholarship to college. He would be the first member of his family to attend college. That prospect would disappear if Bud changed schools. So my parents agreed to take him in for his senior year.

Financially this was a big strain on my family. Mom had just finished college, was paying off student loans, and had just gotten a job teaching. Dad's salary as a high school football coach and teacher was around $3500 a year. Bud was a big, growing boy who was physically active and ate a lot. In theory, both his parents and the Booster Club would provide us with a supplement to support some of Bud's expenses. For the most part, that support was not forthcoming. Many mornings Lisa, Bud, and I would be sitting at a square white formica and aluminum kitchen table eating our cereal, my mom would be standing at the kitchen sink washing dishes, and gazing out the window as the curtains fluttered. She would casually ask, "Bud, have you spoken with your mother? Is there a check in the mail?"

"Yes ma'am. She said she mailed it Monday."

It rarely arrived.

Bud took us to the playground regularly and pushed us on the merry-go-round until our heads were spinning and we could not walk a straight line. He baby-sat us, engaging us in wrestling matches, and tossing us in the air for our 'airplane' rides. He took a long time in the shower, causing us to line up for the bathroom on weekday mornings. He rode to and from school with my father. He was Daddy's weight lifting buddy in the weight room in our garage. They spotted each other and talked trash.

"Coach, is that the best you can do? You must be getting old," Bud would tease as the whoosh of breath and clanging of weights accompanied Daddy's uplift.

"Bud, I can out press you any day. Add me another 5 pounds on either end," he would say as he settled the bar bells back into their rack.

"Only fives? Need me to get you a protein shake before you press it?"

"Boy, you'd better watch out or I'll tell that girlfriend of yours that you only like her because she's ro-BUST." They would both fall about laughing at dad's joke, and command of the English language.

At the end of that year, Bud graduated high school with a full scholarship to college. We helped him pack up his gear and put him on a bus to Florida, back to his family. For Lisa and I his leaving was sad because we loved having a big brother. But, it was also liberating; we now no longer had to share a bedroom, or queue for the bathroom. For Daddy, Bud's departure meant that his home life reverted to one dominated by females. For Momma, Bud's leaving meant there was one less mouth to feed.

...

As young children, we would regularly go to the Saturday kid's matinee. For fifty cents you could get a movie ticket—a double feature if you were lucky—and a soda with popcorn or a box of candy. On one particular Saturday I had on a new pair of T-strapped sandals. As the movie was ending and I was walking out of the theatre, I stepped on gum. It was horrifying. My shoe was spoiled, and the gum was a stringy sticky pink blob. My mom produced a napkin from the bottom of her purse, and pulled the bubble from the bottom of my shoe. But, long threads of sticky gum remained, causing my shoe to stick to the floor with each step out of the theatre. Once home my mother got a knife and scraped and scraped until nothing remained but a thin patina of clear stickiness, which left a lingering subtle tackiness to my step for weeks.

From that day forward, I have hated gum. I cannot stand to see people chewing it. I can smell that sweet, artificial smell on anyone, anywhere, and it makes me gag. I find it extremely uncomfortable to be in a car or elevator with people chewing it. I have never let my own children partake of it in my presence.

This weakness was one that my older sister exploited. If she really wanted to torture me, she would place a piece of Juicy Fruit or Bubblicious gum inside my pillow case, under my pillow, where I could smell it but not see it, as soon as I got into bed. One night, I went crying to my mother, complaining that the gum smell was so strong I couldn't sleep. She, of course, smelled nothing, and sent me back to bed. We repeated this dance a number of times before Lisa fessed up, retrieving the gum from its hiding place at the bottom of my pillow case, and laughing at my distress.

For all of our youth, if my sister and I were engaged in a truly meaningful competition, Lisa would bet me that I had to chew a piece of gum for one minute if I lost the challenge. The gum bet was a sure sign of the seriousness of our activities. Needless to say, there were a number of occasions where I lost and had to suffer my fate. Such experiences only reinforced my revulsion.

Not only did Lisa best me in the spot-on cruelty of her bets, but she also beat me literally and figuratively in our physical encounters. Quite simply, she possessed the killer instinct, and I did not. As young girls we typically got into conflicts over space, our most contested arenas being the back seat of the car, or the living room couch if we were watching TV. Each of us claimed one side of the back car seat—no bucket seats in those days—depending on which door we entered, and imposed an imaginary line down the middle separating Lisaland from Loriland. Transgressions across the border would lead to physical retaliation with us 'facing' each other with our feet, and engaging in a kicking contest. Even the most peaceful, relaxed moments could descend quickly into war with the smallest slip across the dividing line.

Lisa was the master of heel kick to the shin. Such blows sent shocks through the body and left big, blue bruises the size of silver dollars all up and down the legs. If we were in an especially viscous fight, pinching and biting would be involved. The effectiveness of the pinch was totally dependent on the size and location of the attack. The inner thigh and arm were the optimal location, and a small amount of skin between thumb and index finger was the optimal size. This combination ensured maximum pain. Sometimes, we would bite.

Pinching and kicking were aggressive, warmongering acts, but they would not get you kicked out of nursery school. Biting would. So it was something that my mother absolutely would not tolerate, and she developed an ingenious punishment for it. Once she stopped the fight, she would find out who bit first. Whoever that was had to hold out her arm and let the other one bite it for as long and as hard as she liked. This punishment usually worked in my favor since I was not, as I have said, the aggressive one. However, on the occasions that I would bite first, I was in for a heap of pain, for I knew that Lisa could lay the ivory on you like a cannibal. That was something I just could not do, since the squishiness of the flesh repulsed me, reminding me of the chewiness of gum.

There is only one incident from my childhood that I can remember where I was the true aggressor, and did real damage. We were about twelve and thirteen at the time, the period of my extreme sense of sisterly inferiority. We were home one day alone. A group of kids in the neighborhood came to the door. Lisa answered. They wanted to play. Lisa responded, "Lori can play, but I'm busy." Since they were younger kids, Lisa was palming them off on me. I was so angry that I attacked her on the stairs, and clawed her right across the face. This sent her screaming—after all she was the pretty one—and that frightened those younger kids away. You could say, I killed two birds with one scratch.

CHAPTER 5

Southern (Dis)Comforts

"Flowers may bloom again, but a person never has the chance to be young again. So don't waste your time."

Chinese proverb

"You can discover more about a person in an hour of play than a year of conversation."

Plato

"Men who have lost their heart have not yet won a trophy."

Greek proverb

Since both of my parents worked, Lisa and I spent our preschool years and our after school hours with a couple we called Grandma Daniels and Uncle Pen. Uncle Pen was a thin, matchstick of a man, and Grandma Daniels was a soft, doughy woman. He ran the farm; she drove a school bus. They lived way out in the country. They were kind, country folk who ruled a kingdom of barnyard critters, wild animals, and nature.

I loved to feed the chickens on the farm and watch the way they pecked around in the pen for food. I played 'house' with the kittens, pretending that one was my baby and our home was the back two rows of the school bus that was always parked along the side of the Daniel's front yard. As the evening would come on, Lisa and I would catch lightening bugs and trap them in a jar. We would put grass in the bottom and poke holes in the lid so they could breathe. In the mornings however, they always seemed to be dead.

On a farm, death is always lurking around somewhere. It is present in the dead birds the cat brings to the door step, the dead snake Uncle Pen had to shoot because it got into the chicken coop, the calf that did not make it. But nothing prepares you for the smell and specifics of death like the decapitation of a chicken. Uncle Pen would draw the neck of the chicken across a stump in the barnyard that he kept specifically for this purpose. He would lift the axe as the bird squawked and wiggled to get free. In one swift motion the axe would land with a thump, and catch in the stump. The bird's head would roll to the ground, and Uncle Pen would release the body. It would run wildly around the barnyard, headless, wings flapping, and bleeding from the neck. This macabre scene would last for about twenty to thirty seconds, then the chicken would plop unceremoniously to the ground.

As a child I found this terrifying, yet fascinating. I read once that when the human head is severed from the body the mind still processes for about thirty seconds. I have more than once wondered what I would be thinking about in those last thirty seconds. I do believe that that wildly flapping chicken body is the chicken manifestation of the body/mind continuing to process.

Most children are fascinated by death, the grotesque, and the seemingly abnormal—the flattened dead frog you find in the middle of the street, the dwarf you follow around in the department store, the one-legged man you can't stop looking at, the protruding belly and navel of a pregnant woman, the missing digit of a person's hand, the dead, hard, waxy body of your great grandfather in his coffin. But, what you realize as you grow older is that the preoccupation with death is due to the fact that most people have not been up close and personal with it. Once you have, death either sucks you in to its sweetness, or you want to get as far away as possible.

My most personal youthful encounter with death was that of my pet hamster Elvis. I kept him in a cage on my dresser, and was dedicated to his care and maintenance. He had a little wheel that he loved to run around in, and fresh cedar chips to burrow and nest in. That summer the family went on a vacation to I-know-not-where. As part of the leaving, Momma made me move his cage to the garage with all of Daddy's weights and his lifting bench. We brought Elvis a super duper sized water bottle, and arranged for the neighbors to check his water and feed him. When we got home the hamster was dead. I cried and carried on so that Momma decided we would have a funeral for him to give me closure and comfort.

I got a child's shoe box and lined it with tissue. I placed his limp body in it. The box was white, so I drew a black cross on top with magic marker. Momma and I said a few words while Lisa stood solemnly by. We dug a small hole and buried him under the window to my bedroom beneath a boxwood bush. I mourned at that window, staring at that bush, for days. When I was a young adult, my mother told me that it was only later that she realized the hamster had not been dead after all; it had been in hibernation, because the garage, having no windows, was dark and cool. Some things you are just better off not knowing.

That fall all of America got acquainted with death due to the assassination of John F. Kennedy. It occurred on a weekday and during school hours. We kids got our first inkling that something big was happening when the teachers began to gather in the halls and tear up. Some were crying and carrying on in a way that made us quite afraid. The adults were losing it, and we had no idea why. The general confusion led to early release from school, which only upped our anxiety.

Momma taught at our school so she gathered us up, shared the news, took us home, and turned on the TV, a bulbous black and white set that was perched on a rolling metal stand in the living room. There were only three channels in those days, and the programming ended at midnight with the playing of the national anthem, and waving of the flag. After that, the screen went to black and white confetti. On every channel that day the programming was news updates of President Kennedy's condition—dead by this time—speculation regarding the who and why, and discussion of the lines of presidential succession.

The next morning it was more of the same. Every house had the TV tuned into Walter Cronkite. A general sense of unease settled on all of us. What I recall most vividly from this time was the nervousness that characterized every adult you encountered, made worse by the whispered conversations taking place between them, the inability to discuss anything else, and the elegance and sorrow of Jackie Kennedy. Only my father remained unaffected, for he was a guy who had never even registered to vote because elections took place during the Playing Season, and in his world the Playing Season was all consuming. This fact lent a steadiness to my world that was both comforting and reassuring, given the situation.

I was five, standing in the living room in my lounge wear of white cotton panties, watching the funeral procession with that riderless horse. Jackie's black veil and John John's salute broke my heart. I did not fully understand what was happening, but was afraid and sad about it nonetheless. For me, fear about death would trump sweetness for many years to come.

...

In the early sixties, we lived in Savannah, near the Georgia coast. When you grow up in the South near the coast, you grow up with the smell not exactly of death, but of decay. It seeps up out of the marsh and damp soil into the air. It is a funky, heavy smell that is both comforting—aha, I'm home—and repulsive—my, but that stinks. I have both of these reactions to my native lands. But, for me, this smell connotes arriving; it means welcome home. Home was a place full of swimming, crabbing, tubing, and just plain hanging out on, and in, the coastal waters, and the intercostal marshes and creeks, immersed in that Southern funk.

Tybee Beach was our local beach as young children. The sand was white, the waters were warm, the beaches were wide and segregated. Blacks made camp at the north end of the beach while the white domain was a long stretch to the south. Young black boys would walk the south end selling boiled peanuts in brown paper bags for five cents each. My family could always be counted on to buy at least four bags, one for each of us and, more usually, five, a full quarter's worth. If none of the black boys made the migration south, Daddy and I would walk up to their part of the beach to make our purchase.

I was fascinated by the sight of hundreds of negroes spread out on blankets basking in the sun. I asked my dad on one of these excursions north, "Why are they sunbathing? They're already black." He replied with a chuckle, "They're tanning their palms and feet."

As with sports, you could count on commerce to provide a small bridge across the racial divide. But, unlike sports, no one felt fully satisfied with commercial exchanges. Blacks felt exploited and whites felt embarrassed or debased, depending on their degree of prejudice. In the underbelly of the South, the crossing of the racial divide manifested in small and much more intimate ways that were more fulfilling; the warmth of Nellie's soft bosom and strong arms, the smell of her cornbread cooking in the oven, a laugh shared on the playground; or more frightening; an aggressive brush in the line to the movie theatre, a passive aggressive stare from a car window, an outright threat, "I'm gonna knock your teeth out white girl if you don't get out of here."

Outside of the wonderful salty, wet taste of a boiled peanut, one of the most powerful and joyful memories I have of my childhood is crabbing. It was akin to a religious experience. To me it was more holy than church or Sunday school. Football being religion in the South and Daddy's position as the local high priest of high school football—head coach—meant that we got invited to many of the homes of team boosters, players, and their families for crabbing days and other get togethers on the salt water creeks of the intercoastal waterways.

We would arrive about noon with casseroles, desserts, and chips in hand, and beer in the cooler. There would be long picnic tables set up in the backyard which sloped gently down to the dock and the creek. Typically the tables would be covered in newspaper and placed end to end so they appeared to be one of those endless tables you see in movies about kings and knights. There would be nutcrackers placed intermittently all along the table, and benches strung along each side for seating. A competitive game of horseshoes would be in progress along the side yard.

Daddy would jump right into that competition. "I'll play the winner. I sure hope that's you, Peanut, with those scrawny arms," he would say as he was popping open a beer and throwing his head back for that first sip. "Can I grab you one?"

"No thanks Lamar. I'm not drinkin'."

"Aw Peanut, you're nothing but a boring Lutheran. At least we Baptists know how to sin now, and repent later."

Most importantly, though, would be the smell of crab boil rising from at least one and, more likely, two or three large cauldrons heating up over low fires. If you have never smelled crab boil, it has a salty, spicy, peppery fragrance that I love to this day. I have been known to buy Old Bay Seasoning as a proxy for that smell. Mingle the scent with the funk of the creek and marsh, and the sweat of men's bodies, and you have one of the most alluring smells on the planet for a real Southern girl.

The kids would be running and jumping off the dock and tubing in the creek. All along the dock would be secured pieces of old, dried wood wound with strings that were dangling in the water. These would be the crabbing lines with chicken necks, gizzards, and other throw-away parts secured at their ends. Nets with long handles would be placed strategically and intermittently along the dock. As soon as you saw a line go taut you would grab a net, and slowly, very slowly ease the string up. If you were lucky or good, you would scoop up a crab or two. And, if you were a young child, crabbing was a type of fishing that you could be good at because all it required was for you to watch, wait, and ask for help, if you needed it. All the catch then went into large pails of creek water. As the day progressed and the catch mounted, those pails looked like a moving, swirling mess of red, white, and blue. God bless America!

People peeled off layers as the day progressed into heat. My dad was always looking for an excuse to take his shirt off and show off his pecs and biceps, so fun in the sun was right up his alley. Within an hour or two of his arrival he could be counted on to be shirtless and sweaty. He would rub his chest, flexing his biceps as he bantered with his mates.

"Deke, what happened to the honey we saw you with last Friday night? Did you meet her Mokie? She's what I like to term ro-BUST. You know what I mean?"

"Lamar, you know Deke's only interested in her for her brains. Ain't that right Deke?"

Once the sun was low in the sky, all the kids were sunburnt, and the adults were sufficiently loose and relaxed, the fires would be cranked up a notch and crabs would be dropped live into the boiling water. We, the children, took great pleasure in being able to assist in the dumping and stirring since we had no awareness of issues of animal cruelty, PETA did not even exist, and animal death did not count if you ate it. We were helping, and we were proud of it. The adults would assume their positions at the table, and batch by batch, boiled crab would be scooped out of the pots with wire baskets, and dumped at intervals down the middle. This is the point where the voices got louder, the children wilder, and the lies bigger.

Every so often we kids would run up to the table, open our mouths like baby birds, and be rewarded with a mouthful of sweet, salty crab. We would then resume our game of Hide and Seek, War, or Red Rover, Red Rover. When we got tired of that we would get jars and commence the competition to collect the most lightening bugs.

On the intercoastal waterways at night there were more lightening bugs in those days than you could shake a stick at, and not one bit of ambient light. On a moonless night the sky was blue-black, and the stars and fireflies sparkled like diamonds. Moon or no, the sky was a beautiful and magical sight. The abundance of fireflies made the darkness less threatening, and the night a child's fairyland. When we were satisfied with our catch, we would fall where we stood in the grass and watch the light show of twinkling stars and lightening bugs above us. Many a child fell into such a deep and restful sleep in that grass that her parents had to pull out the flashlights to search for her when it was time to finally go home.

At outings such as these, nicknames were both creative and common. There was at least one Cooter—always male to my recollection, that says something right there—as well as Pokey, Stumpy, Moodie, Mokie, Sweet Pea, Sweet Thang, Honey Pie, Junior, Hoss, Radar, Cup Cake, Sugar, Squirt, and Sug. JP, PJ, JR, RJ, JT, JC, CJ, CT, TJ, RC, and an array of other initial names were also common. Usually the nicknames were based on some physical characteristic or act of great accomplishment or great humiliation, while the use of initials was an effort to distinguish the offspring—JT—from the parent—James Thomas.

My daddy was a frequent bestower of nicknames. In part, this talent reflected his sense of humor. Since men and women wanted to bask in his light, if they received such a gift from him they cherished it. Once bestowed, they used it. When he was coaching college ball he had nicknames for all of his players. At South Carolina he called one of his boys Hollywood due to his perpetual tan and perfect hair. Another was referred to as Hec Ramsey, after the TV show of that name, and because both the young man and Richard Boone, the actor in the series, had Fu Manchu mustaches. In his early pro coaching days Daddy had a colleague he nicknamed the Reptile because the guy never seemed to sweat. He called the sun the big eye, an attractive woman a honey, and me LuLu. In return, we called him The Dude, a term we coined long before *The Big Lebowski* seared it into public consciousness. Lisa, not being the nickname type, never got or wanted one.

The fall brought more ritualized fun on the intercoastal. Family friends had built a cinderblock, screened-in barbecue pit and adult playroom of sorts right by the creek. In hunting season, the men would hang out there, dressing the meat, grilling venison, and playing ping pong as the sun set. The children would be inside playing at the back of the house under the supervision of a baby sitter or older sibling. The women would be moving between the playroom and the house, ferrying beer and other necessities back and forth. On days like these, everyone had a predetermined role and a slow, easy rhythm, as naturally predetermined as man's mastery over beast, and as easy as a sashay.

Once everyone had had their fill of sizzling deer meat, the living room would be cleared, the music would be cranked up, a broomstick would appear, and a wild contest of limbo would commence. My mother loved that game since she was quite good at it. Daddy took great pride in her abilities, especially since it was a game he absolutely could not play due to his football knee injuries. He admired her flexibility and rhythm. He thought her sexy as she slid below the broom moving to the beat of the music, her auburn flip brushing the floor, her tight top slipping up to expose her mid-section, and her white peddle pushers straining over her thighs and pubis. He would encouragingly say, "That's right baby, you've got this. A little lower Paula. A little lower."

...

In 1964, our time in the deep, coastal South came to an end. Daddy was leaving Jenkins High School over a dispute with the Booster Club regarding support for the team, and his demanding ways. He was still upset over the lack of support we had received when we took Bud in for a year. When he instituted an extra practice to the daily schedule and parents complained to the principal, that was it. He resolved to get into college coaching. He took a position coaching at Key West High School while he began to work on, and build, his network. This began the nomadic period of our lives; some might term it my dad's professional ascent.

To make the move, my dad enlisted the aid of a couple of his players from Jenkins High School. They packed that U-Haul with all our worldly possessions, including Daddy's weights, and hitched it to the car. We loaded ourselves in. Daddy started the engine and gave it some gas. The front wheels of the car promptly separated from the asphalt, and we girls in the back seat had the sensation of flying. Some strategic renegotiation took place between Momma and Daddy, things in the back were rearranged and left behind—not the weights of course—and off we went.

We arrived in Florida in mid-summer in time to get settled before the start of Pre-season and the school year. In short order it was the Playing Season and hurricane season. When hurricane season comes to southern Florida, everyone gets busy. Folks stock up on bottled water, sterno, and lots of canned goods. My family was late to this game, as we were novices with respect to hurricanes, and had never been campers. However, as our first hurricane set its eye on the Florida coast, Momma laid in the supplies and moved her car to higher ground. Daddy, never a handyman, bought large, unwieldy pieces of plywood and got busy himself boarding up all the windows of our little white and green frame bungalow.

When the hurricane came, it blew in with a vengeance. For three days and nights the winds whipped the palm trees, the rain poured steady and hard, beating against the house in a rhythmic, hypnotic way. Days and nights became virtually indistinguishable. A couple of times a day we would crack the front door to peer outside and gauge the progress of the rising water levels.

Those door cracks were the most exciting thing to punctuate the hours. With the windows boarded up and no electricity—that had gone out some time during the first day of the storm—we were living by candlelight, on canned goods, cereal, no milk, and bottled water. Lisa and I played every board game we had, while Momma and Daddy smoked, and played cards. At first it felt like a real adventure. But, as the days wore on we all tired of one another, and our limited entertainment options. On day four, the water level was cresting the second step from the top of the front porch, but then the rains stopped, and winds mercifully abated. Everyone threw open their doors and began hollering and greeting their neighbors up and down the street.

As Daddy emerged from the dark cave of the house, he spotted our neighbor across the street fiddling with the motorized engine on the back of his small metal boat, "Jack, you gonna crank that thing up? Have you been out in it yet? How do things look?"

"Don't know Lamar, I'm getting ready to head out now. You want to come along to check things out?"

"You, bet. Got any beer?" Daddy was yelling like an excited boy just getting released from school.

Native Floridians kept small boats for fishing, which they employed to cruise the streets after the floods. If you were lucky, or well liked, they would motor to your porch in flood times and offer you a shot of whiskey, a beer, or better yet, a ride. The atmosphere was one of a low-rent, week-long party. Daddy got more than a few rides during the week that the water stayed high and the power off. The rest of us remained housebound, hollering and carrying on from the front stoop.

Once the water receded, the mess and the stink were awful. Dead fish, seaweed, uprooted palms, and various other trees and shrubs, coconuts, bicycles, and all manner of children's toys, tools, and other small items, littered the streets and yards. Mud and sand packed the parking lots and ditches. In the trees that remained standing, I spotted naked dolls, rags, and more dead sea life.

It was as if the ocean had been turned inside out. In the weeks that followed, my playmates and I found tiny, shriveled-up sea horses, desiccated fish, bits of coral, and whole coconuts in the ditches along the sides of our street. We cracked those coconuts and drank their sweet milk, while we poked and turned the dead sea life with sticks so that we could examine their structure and composition. We flicked dead dried out carcasses at each other, and buried others.

Given all of the destruction, no one living in Key West at the time completely escaped the hurricane season without loss. Ours was Momma's Cadillac. It was a beautiful champagne colored number, and was the first in the MaMa Cadillac series. While we had moved our cars to higher ground, the flood level had surpassed all projections, and salt water had corroded its innards. It too was dead.

It was during this year in Florida that I had my first real exposure to music. Everyone at my school was required to take lessons. I was not opposed to this idea, but I was very clear about what instrument I wanted to play—the drums. I was told that the drums were an instrument that only boys played; apparently, in the 1960s, only boys had rhythm. I was given a recorder and required to attend lessons every Tuesday morning along with a number of other girls. By the end of that year the only thing that I could play was *The Old Grey Goose Is Dead.*

When we moved again, I never returned to music education or appreciation, something I regret. In my home there simply was no music, or foreign language, or anything to train the ear, or the brain, with respect to sound. Of course we had a record player, but my parents rarely listened to music, and if they did, it was always and only country. It would still be years before Lisa and I bought our first albums at the Walgreens. So I grew up tone-deaf and linguistically challenged, which was a real impediment to my youthful ambition of becoming a rock star.

Swimming lessons with Daddy

PART II

Training Camp or Pre-season

This season occurs in the summer. Like spring leading into summer in the traditional calendar, Training Camp, or Pre-season, precedes the Playing Season. It is filled with sweat and pain, preparation and anticipation.

CHAPTER 6

Moving Up and Out

"If you don't have a plan for yourself, you'll be part of someone else's."

American proverb

"The person who removes a mountain begins by carrying away small stones."

Chinese proverb

"Most men die from the neck up at twenty-five because they stop dreaming."

Ben Franklin

In 1960, while he was coaching high school ball, Daddy was asked to return to professional ball and play for what would become the New York Jets. Momma was thrilled, since the pay involved a substantial upgrade. She urged him to take the job. He refused. When asked later why, he stated quite profoundly, "Why would I want to continue to abuse my body that way? And after all, I enjoy working with young men as a coach and teacher." So in 1965, when Daddy landed a job at the University of Richmond coaching the Spiders, all of us were thrilled. After our year-long sojourn in Florida, all of the networking had paid off, and dad's professional ascent had begun.

At Richmond he coached under Frank Jones who was the head coach, and with Dale Haupt who, like Daddy, eventually ended up in the NFL with a Super Bowl ring. So we loaded up the U-Haul and, for the second time in as many years, moved far away—this time to Richmond, Virginia.

Our time in Richmond would last only two years, but I remember it as idyllic. We bought a charming two-story, white frame house on a wooded cul-de-sac. It had dormer windows, a screened-in side porch with tile flooring, a slate patio, and my mother built a fish pond in the backyard. Mother, who had always possessed a sense of style and panache, fixed it up into a postcard-perfect little nest. She enlisted our help to paint the interior—we did the bottom half of the walls, she did the top, and all of the trim work. She then filled the house with a great variety of junk shop finds, the most impressive of which was a beautiful walnut dining room set that she bought for $32 at auction, and that she still dines on today.

This move to Richmond was the sixth move Momma had organized and orchestrated since she and Daddy had married. By this time she knew what could be accomplished with a can of paint, and how to integrate quickly into a neighborhood. By the second or third day in a new place, Momma would take Lisa by one hand and me by the other, and set off down the block. She would march the three of us up the walks, and knock on the front doors of house after house.

"Hello, I'm Paula Leachman. These are my girls, Lisa and Lori. We just moved in around the corner, at 1228 Hill Circle," she would say to whomever answered the door. "Do you have any children?"

She did not wait for us to find our mates and our groove. She thrust us into the nucleus of our new environments. That environment in Richmond was a quiet cul-de-sac, with three children our age across the circle. It was this child's paradise. We could ride our bikes without oversight, play where we wanted with friends, and generally be free. Lisa and I were no longer stuck with just each other as playmates.

During our neighborhood play dates we played 'house' a lot. We would make the boundaries of our houses and delineate the rooms with straw and rocks. Across the circle, Allison, Hillary, and Eric's back yard was our 'neighborhood.' Found objects would serve as furniture and decoration; an upturned paint can might be a stool, a towel was a bed. My doll would be my child and, if I was the lucky one, Eric, the only boy, would be my baby daddy. Otherwise I would have to pretend, if I cared enough to make the effort. When I did, I would pretend my baby daddy was away for an out-of-town game, or on the road recruiting.

"Hillary, can Baby Suzie and Baby Gail have a play date?" I said as I perched Baby Suzie on my right hip and cocked it to the side. "Bob's out of town since Richmond is playing Ole Miss this weekend, and I'm just fed up with entertaining this baby. I didn't get one wink of sleep last night because she had me up and down, up and down, up and down," I added with a sigh.

"Well Lori, I think that'll work," Hillary would say as she pretended to tidy up her living room by sweeping dirt and pebbles out the 'front door,' " but you'll need to collect Susie by four since Eric will be home for dinner tonight. I'm plannin' on fixin' somethin' special. His favorite—steak with a baked potato."

"You know Hillary, that's Bob's favorite too." I would say, nodding knowingly. "Do you know a man who doesn't like steak and potatoes?" Hillary and I would toss our hair around and affect the knowing laugh we heard our mothers use.

Other days we would play kickball in the circle, or create a bike riding contest of one form or another.

"The goal of this game is to see who's the fastest," Lisa would say. "You have to ride your bike to the end of the circle, around that bucket, and back here around the starting line four times. If you fall or put your foot on the ground you have to start over. Everybody ready? Allison, you say go."

...

During this period, in addition to dogs, which we have always had, and bred, and raised, I got a pet rabbit for my birthday. Her name was Rose Bud. She was white, with black spots and floppy ears. My mother made me keep her in the free standing garage that was at the back of the yard. There she had a large cozy cardboard box to call home. One day when I was playing with Rose Bud, instead of Allison, Hillary, and Eric, I decided that she needed some windows in her home so she could eyeball like Grandpa Leachman liked to do. I got a pair of scissors and cut a variety of different sized and shaped windows in her box. The next day when I went out to the garage to play with her, she was gone. She had chewed holes where all the windows had been, and hopped off into never-never land. Between Rose Bud and the hamster, I decided then and there that small, cage dwelling animals were not things that I could nurture or keep.

Around this time I broke my arm at school one day playing kickball. Kickball was one of my favorite playground games because I was decent at it, and therefore did not get picked last when we were dividing up the teams. That day it was my turn to kick and I hit the ball straight on, and started my run to first base. One of the other players corralled the ball and threw it at me to tag me out. It hit me at my feet, knocking them out from under me. I broke my fall with my left hand, landing hard on the asphalt. That was it, snap!

Right away I knew I was really hurt, but I was so concerned with the fact that my skirt had flown up, my panties were showing, and I had ripped holes in my fishnet tights, that the full effects of my injuries did not register right away. Never underestimate the power of embarrassment to trump pain in a prideful person.

I was taken to the office and given a cot to lay down on. Since my mom was a teacher, the school nurse said, "Lori. Your mom will be in to get you as soon as school's out." I laid there alone in the silence for hours registering the painful throbbing of my arm, and knowing that I needed to see a doctor. Fortunately, I still had my right hand thumb to suck for comfort. When I finally did get to the doctor, I had serious breaks in two places near the wrist.

As my mother and I sat in the doctor's office, he informed her that I would need a cast for more than six weeks due to the severity of the breaks.

"I really had no idea her injury was that serious," Mom said. She turned her gaze to me and stroked my hair saying, "Oh Lori honey, I'm so sorry I made you wait."

That evening when my dad got home he asked what happened. As I was explaining, he said, "Well, did you at least make it to first base?" I truthfully responded, "No." I could sense this was not an optimal answer, but it was all I had to give him.

I wore that cast for three months, through the summer, covered in plastic, secured with rubber bands, so I could go to the pool. Each iteration was appropriately signed and decorated with graffiti. By the time each cast was replaced with a new one, the edges across the palm and thumb especially would be crumbled and fraying. By the time I got it off permanently, my left wrist and forearm were weirdly smaller than the right.

...

Due to the brotherhood that is football, our best childhood friends in Richmond were the four offspring of the head coach Frank, and his wife Jean: Page, Brad, Frank Jr. and Boo, Little Jeanie. Our times together typically took place at their house due to the size of their brood and the delightful, anything goes nature of their house.

They had the messiest house I have ever seen in my entire life. Big Jean made no apologies for this. She had grown up as Southern royalty in a large house with a cook and maids. Big Jean was the daughter of a man named Wally Butts—a football legend. He was the head coach at the University of Georgia for decades as well as the athletic director from 1939 to 1963.

During the two years we lived in Richmond, Big Jean, all too aware of the peripatetic nature of a football coach's life, never bothered to unpack all the boxes of books, many of the toys or linens, or a multitude of other paraphernalia the family had moved to Richmond. This meant that one of the upstairs bedrooms made for ideal fort material. We used those boxes, and books, and stuff to create a labyrinth of tunnels and secret spaces. We used towels and sheets to create roofs for our dwellings so the boys could not spy on us. All six of us had our own private space within the larger community; we were really ahead of the curve with respect to the co-housing movement. And, because two of our partners in play were rowdy boys, we also managed to bust holes in the walls to connect the two upstairs bedrooms and make a short 'slide' over the ceiling of the stairwell.

When the thrill ran out on the indoor play we moved to the roof. The boys rigged up a landing pad of sorts from old lounge chair cushions and a discarded mattress, below the eave of the back roof. We then dragged mattresses and pillows to the peak and slid off. Depending on your weight and wind up, you could gain some real air time and sail to a landing on the pad below. Somehow, none of us ever broke an arm or a leg. We were tough kids. We were coaches' kids.

You might wonder where our parents were while this activity was in progress. Well, the men were working, or working out, and the ladies were inside having a cocktail. Cocktail hour was any hour when the families got together. Instinctively we understood and appreciated this as children. It made the ladies languid and loose, and gave us the liberty to be the wild animals that we were.

None of the football wives and mothers that I remember were Donna Reed or Martha Stewart types, although some were definitely more crafty and homey than others. My impression as a young child was that these women were either high-powered women, in charge of everything but football, like my mother, or they were what I would now call high maintenance women, like Jean Jones. Jean did not do housework and rarely cooked. She did not closely monitor her children or care if their beds were made. She did get her hair done and paint her nails.

My mother on the other hand, had certain rules that kept us straight and kept her many family duties in check. For example, every morning our beds had to be made and our teeth and hair had to be brushed before we could leave the house. In addition, my family never owned a lawn mower; my mother knew that if we did, mowing the lawn would become woman's work. Mother also never developed any proficiency with anything mechanical or electrical. If she had, she would have been expected to be able to fix all manner of broken things rather than hire help. Such a task would have been nearly impossible, given that we never even had a tool box. We had a hammer, some nails, and a screwdriver in a drawer in the kitchen.

Momma was not a sewer, knitter, or gardener. Similarly, she knew that if she was a great cook we would go out to eat less often. So, she had seven dishes that she was good at. She said, "Seven is plenty. If company plans to stay longer then they should be taking us out to eat." She never baked, and she only cooked special requests on our birthdays. The introduction of squeeze butter absolutely revolutionized her time in the kitchen. "Here, have a shot of butter," she would say, or "It's not done yet, I haven't added the butter," or "That meat looks dry, here, squeeze a bit of butter on it." Nothing, however, could ever improve her laundry skills. We wore tie dye in our household long before, and after, it was hip.

To give you an even more complete sense of how unrefined our culinary experiences were, during football season on Thursday nights, our special treat was a dine in dinner at Arby's. Arby's Roast Beef had just come to Richmond and Lisa and I loved it. We would both order a small roast beef sandwich with fries and a coke, and sit at the same corner table every week as we ate. That table afforded us the most complete view of all of the folks entering, ordering, and exiting, thereby enabling us to eyeball throughout dinner. If we had had a particularly good week or day, we might even get dessert for dinner in the form of a milkshake.

During football season Daddy ate at the training table with the team, since steak was always on the menu, and he would work until at least ten or eleven every night leading up to a game. In the off season when he was with us, our special dine out treat was dinner at Gus's Italian. Gus's was a small, dark pizza and pasta place with celebrity caricatures on the wall, and crayons for kids. You could bring your own bottle, and customize your music by playing the juke box. Lisa and I would share an order of Spaghetti a la Gus while listening to Nancy Sinatra sing *These Boots Are*

Made for Walking. As the evening wore on, Momma and Daddy would slow dance in the darkness, silhouetted by the neon from the juke box to *Ode to Billie Joe, You've Lost that Loving Feeling,* or *Light My Fire,* while us girls finished our coloring masterpieces or playing a competitive game of Hangman. We could have a full evening out for four for under ten dollars including the tip.

Our lack of cultural refinement extended beyond the culinary domain and into the artistic. As young children Lisa and I never went to an art museum unless it was on a school field trip. Museums were something that my father had little interest in, and when he was present, our time and energy were focused on things that we could do together as a family that he would enjoy. This meant our family time featured outings such as boating, swimming, crabbing, attending other sports' events, or playing putt-putt golf and the like. When he was not present, it was the Playing Season—enough said.

During one highly competitive game of putt-putt, mom and dad played Lisa and me.

"Hot damnit, Paula. Can't you hit the ball straighter than that? You're ruining our score," Daddy said, as he watched mom's ball skip over the border of the third hole and roll to a stop by the tenth.

"Lamar, if you don't like the way I play, you can be a team of one. Girls, can I be on your team?" she said, twirling her golf club as she turned to us.

"Yeah! It'll be the girls against the boy," we clapped.

And so it was. The final score? Boy–42, Girls–184.

Our high culture events featured drive-in movies. In these early years we went to the drive-in alot. You paid by the car— two dollars—and did not need to hire a baby sitter. The end of this tradition occurred during our first years in Atlanta. One night our family went to see a double feature. The opening film was a western of some sort, which my father loved. However, my parents were really there for the second showing, *Barbarella.* The expectation was that Lisa and I would be asleep in the back by the time it came on. However, once we spied the far out nature of the film, we took turns sneaking peeks of the screen over the front seat.

"Girls, lay down and go to sleep. Paula, I thought you said they'd be asleep by now."

"Well, I thought they would Lamar. Do you want to leave?"

"No. Damn it. I want to see the movie. Don't you?"

"Yes, I do. Girls, if I catch you sneaking peaks again I am going to dock your allowance fifty cents."

Money or not, the film was too enticing to ignore. When I caught the scene of Jane inhaling the essence of man from a water pipe, I thought I knew exactly what that was about, since I had spent plenty of time in locker rooms over the years. I was totally confused as to why anyone would seek that out, much less consume it.

Daddy's upbringing was totally devoid of any exposure to the higher cultural arts. In addition, the fact that my father was color blind along the red and green spectrum, probably contributed in a meaningful way to his lack of interest in art. Similarly, my mother's exposure to art and music was limited. However, she was a teacher, so we did take trips to the Smithsonian Science Museums during our time in Richmond, in conjunction with family visits to my Aunt Patty's. It was not until we were young adults and Daddy was coaching for the New York Giants that we actually made our first visits to the array of New York art institutions and museums. On every excursion my father would come in with us, look at a few things depending on the establishment, then say, "I think I'll go sit on the bench in the lobby. I'll wait for you there." Or, "We passed a restaurant on the way in. I'll have a beer and meet you there when you're done."

...

In the spring of our first year in Richmond, the Jones household was hosting a very large cocktail party for the coaching staff, athletic department, and boosters. This was a challenge, given the chaotic nature of their home, so Frank Jones enlisted the help of some of his graduate assistant coaches to get the house ready. They arrived with tools in hand to put the toilet seats back on the johns, move furniture and boxes out of the public space, and aid Big Jean in her clean up efforts. However, their help was not enough. Big Jean hired all six of us children—five really, as Boo was too small to be of real help—for a quarter apiece to clean the kitchen. This was no small task since the kitchen had never been cleaned, or so it seemed, in the entire time they had lived there.

Dishes, pots, pans and the like were piled everywhere. Some had been sitting for days? weeks? months? even, with their contents hardened and cemented to the various surfaces. Red sauce of some sort formed a desiccated border around the top of a metal pan. Hardened and dried-out macaroni covered the bottom of a baking dish. Something green stuck to the sides of another. Crusted plates were stacked in four different piles. Silverware was piled in the bottom of the sink. Many of the forks had unidentifiable hardened matter between the prongs. Cups were stacked everywhere. Many contained solidified milk in their bottoms. The trash can was an abomination.

All of us worked for hours, starting at the top and progressing slowly through one pile after another. As an adult I have to ask myself how one family could have had so much kitchenware, but I concluded that when you never clean, you've got to constantly be acquiring new gear. About half way through our task, all of us began to realize that we needed a raise; the grease, grime, and volume of the mess were more than we had bargained for. Collectively, we approached Momma and Big Jean, who were sitting at the dining table with cocktails in hand. In my mother's free hand was her usual cigarette. She held the brown filter between her index and pointer fingers in a pistol grip, the burning end of her cigarette her bullet. The smoke at the tip was swirling up and away from her hand, and around her head like she had just fired a shot. She slowly exhaled, releasing a steady, cloudy stream into the space between us.

"Momma," Paige said to Big Jean, "this is a lot of work. I think we deserve more than a quarter apiece."

"Really? Most of that mess is the by-product of feeding you, so I think it's only right you clean it up." Jean took a leisurely sip of her drink, and scanned our faces.

"But Lisa and Lori didn't eat all this food, or drink from all those glasses."

"You know Paige, you're right. Lisa, Lori, I'll pay you a dollar each." A smile as tight as spandex crossed her face as she combed through her brown hair with manicured nails, and then proceeded to light her own cigarette.

"But what about Paige, and Brad, and Frankie, and Boo?" I asked distressed by my perception of the unfairness of that response.

"They made the mess, they can help clean it up," Big Jean replied.

"How 'bout we all get fifty cents?" said Paige. "It still totals the $3 you would spend by paying Lisa and Lori a dollar, and the rest of us a quarter."

"Only if the girls agree," said Jean.

"Deal," Lisa and I replied in unison.

Our collective bargaining tactics earned us a 100% raise, and that kitchen was never as clean again.

Richmond was a lovely town then and the campus of the University of Richmond was picturesque. Lisa and I would go with Daddy often to the office and play on the track field while he lifted weights. We especially loved all those piles of landing foam behind the pole vaulting bars. If you got your speed up running down the track and executed the perfect leap and twirl, the sensation was like flying through the air—an appreciation our roof top endeavors at Big Jean's had honed in us—and landing in marshmallows.

If we weren't playing around the track and weight room, we were grading a game film or analyzing a competing team in order to share some Daddy time. My father would set up a projector, play the black and white picture on the wall of the kitchen or dining room, and Lisa or I would sit by his side on chairs from the kitchen or dining room tables. We would become hypnotized by the players moving forwards, and then backward as my dad would hit the play and reverse buttons, all the while taking copious notes—set after set of X's and O's on a legal pad, with arrows indicating direction and movement. On occasion, I would have my own paper and make my own notes with crayon, patterning X's and O's into a pyramid or some other form.

"What you got there LuLu?" my dad would ask as he was changing the reel.

"Same thing as you, only prettier."

I do not ever recall a time when my father read to me or my sisters. Grading film was our quiet time and sharing ritual. But, by the end of fourth grade dad was moving up and we were moving on, resulting in an end of these shared activities.

...

It was while we lived in Richmond that we got to go on our second plane ride ever. We knew this was big stuff because we still recalled our first plane ride when I was about four and Lisa was five. We had flown from Savannah, Georgia, to Nashville, Tennessee, to see MaMa. For that trip Momma brought us matching new blue dresses with white round buttons at the shoulder, and white gloves. We wore those gloves and dresses with our black patent leather Mary Janes, and lace trimmed ankle socks. When we stepped off that plane I recall feeling important. The sun was shining, the wind was moving across my skin, and I could see up, out, over, and beyond. I could see MaMa waving at us from the tarmac—this was in the days before security concerns kept friends and family from meeting the disembarking passengers.

As we descended the stairs, MaMa met us. She kissed mom, took Lisa and me by the hands, and escorted us to a fancy lunch at the restaurant in the airport. We ate in a plush, padded, circular booth watching planes take off and land. We were waited on by men in ties. In this day and age one only eats airport food if you can't avoid it, but in 1962, the airport restaurant was a destination, and an experience.

Our second airplane ride was a charter with the University of Richmond football team. The Spiders were playing Mississippi State in Starkville, Mississippi. The team chartered two planes for the team, staff, families and press. In those days football really was a family affair; being a football family was akin to being part of the Astronauts' Wives Club. Every family knew that they represented not only themselves, but the team and the school. So, just like with our trip to Nashville, flying, especially with the team, was a formal affair. Mother informed us, "Girls, you know we'll be flying with the team. This means no pants. Dresses or skirts, and knee socks or tights." In fact, football and all the surrounding ceremony, were formal affairs. Throughout our childhood we were never allowed to wear blue jeans to a game, or dress in anything approaching a casual manner. It was a matter of image and respect as far as my father was concerned.

Once we arrived in Starkville, our planes were met on the tarmac with chartered buses to take us to the stadium. The team and coaches then separated from the families to begin their game day preparations. The families and press were escorted to a large lounge area where food and drinks were waiting. All of us milled around, and grazed, and smoked, and played tag. When it was finally time to take our seats in the stadium, our mothers herded us out and into the designated friends and family section. Our call to attention was the playing of the national anthem. To this day, the playing of the national anthem before any sporting event fills me with patriotism. It makes the hair stand up on my head. The national anthem is followed by the coin toss, which is followed by the kick off, which is followed by physical contact, cheering, and moaning.

My attention was always divided between the game being played on the field and my dad coaching on the sidelines. I loved the way a perfectly timed play unfolded on the field—every man hitting their spot with speed and enthusiasm. I loved the beautiful arc that a perfectly thrown spiral made. I loved it when our defense sacked their quarterback, or our running back left their defenders in the dust. I loved following Daddy sashay up and down the sidelines yelling, "Get-em! Get-em! Get-em!" I loved the players' embodiment of the will to win. I loved the honor in a well fought game. I appreciated the pageantry of the half time show and the spectacle of sport. In short, for me football embodied all that was great about America.

I do not recall whether we won or lost that game in Starkville. What I do recall is being terrified on the ride home. It was late at night and the planes were caught in heavy storms—lots of thunder and lightening—and us right dead in the center of it. I was buckled in my seat by the window with a full view of the wrath of the Gods. Thunder was booming across the sky, shaking the plane. The wings were flapping like birds wings, only more slowly. This seemed totally unnatural to me. The plane was dipping, and rising, and dropping, and rising again. I was sweating and praying as only a naïve believer could.

"Please God, let us land safely. I promise I will read my Bible every night, and pay attention in Sunday School."

"Please God, get us home. I promise I will not be jealous of my sister."

"Please God, save us all. I promise I will love my mother more, and not want Big Jean to be my real mom."

When we landed, I knew I had been delivered by Divine Intervention, for all of us from the Deep South know that football is next to God's heart. After all, America prays before, after, and during every game; the players cross themselves and give thanks to the Lord for their big plays; and, the losses are surely God's will delivered to teach us all a lesson.

I understood early, but not precisely in any way that I could articulate at the time, that my family was part of a very special cult. Today I can define it as the cult of sport and celebrity. But, in those days, it was simply a special, built-in network, generating immediate connection to place through the identification with the team, and allowing a passageway to acceptance into school cliques—though full acceptance was never easy, because girls and social situations never are. The next best thing to being a Baptist preacher in the South is being a football coach. Blessedly the glow of their specialness extends to family and friends. Praise God. Amen.

...

My daddy was an athlete through and through, a man's man. There was nothing he did physically that he did not throw himself into completely. He had a handsome face that improved with age, the kind of face that gives men an unfair advantage. His hair was brown, and once he passed the age of forty, prematurely grey, which only improved his look. He was six feet two inches tall and built like a professional body builder from the waist up. In that he had developed the first iteration of the weightlifting program that most universities continue to use today, he was a walking billboard for his methods.

From the waist down however, he was slim hipped, knocked-kneed, and scarred from his football injuries. So scarred in fact, that he descended stairs sideways, like a crab, leaning heavily on the railing. When he was younger, he had a bit of a hop to his descent, so the peculiar nature of his gait was less noticeable. His injuries meant that he did not have fully functioning knees, so he could not squat or kneel without help.

One Sunday in our first spring in Richmond, we went church shopping. Mom decided we would try the Episcopal Church with the modern sanctuary. At the first prayer that required kneeling and bowing your head, we all assumed the position. When the prayer was over we all rose and sat back in our seats, except Daddy. He could not get up. The space was too tight for him to work himself around into another position where he could negotiate around his knee issues. Likewise, it was too tight for him to use his arms to lever himself back into the seat without changing the position of his legs. We all thought he was just caught up and engaged with the Spirit until he started hissing under his breath, "Paula, I need help. Paula, pull me up. Hot damnit Paula, I can't get up. I'm stuck." With Momma anchoring the left side, and us two girls pulling from the right, the three of us eventually managed to drag him up and into a sitting position. When we left that service Momma joked, "Well Lamar, I guess they're going to think that you're truly repentant. A real holy guy." We never attended an Episcopal service again.

Daddy walked with a heavy foot, heel first, and had a tight little swagger. His walk was always accompanied by the swishing sound of his inner thighs gliding past one another due to his knocked knees. His combination of injuries and anatomy meant that he no longer did sports that required agility and speed, quite simply because he could not be good at them. So, by his thirties, golf became his recreational sport of choice.

Being the competitive soul that he was, he dedicated himself to improving his game in his free time. That meant that he liked to practice his swing. One way that he did this while getting in some quality family time was to have us girls stand way back across the span of the front yard while he hit golf balls at us. We thought this was great because when Daddy was aiming for you, you had his undivided attention.

"LuLu, heads up. It's coming your way," he yelled as the ball flew over my head and through the hedge that separated our yard from the neighbors. "Get-em! Get-em! Get-em! Don't lose it."

"Lisa, this ball's for you."

"Girls, did you see where that landed? Over in the bushes on the right. Crawl up under there and see if you can find it. It's one of my good balls."

One day during practice time my dad placed his ball on the tee. He took a few air strokes to loosen up.

"LuLu, today we start with you. You ready?"

"Yep."

He drew a bead on me which made me stand up straight and proud. Daddy settled into his stance, took a few short half strokes, and hit the ball. BAM! Before I knew what happened that ball drove into my midsection with such force that I lost my breath, jackknifed, and dropped to the ground clutching my stomach. For a few seconds that seemed like minutes, I was incapable of making a sound. When I finally managed to suck in a breath out came a scream, and tears.

Momma came running out of the house. "What happened Lamar? Lori, are you OK?"

"Sure she is, Paula. I just hit her with a golf ball. I think my game is really improving."

"Lamar! You could have knocked her unconscious! Or put her eye out! Or broken her teeth! You are never, and I mean never, to hit golf balls around the girls again."

And he didn't. I kind of missed it, and the undivided attention.

...

By the time I was eight or nine, I knew my daddy was a big believer in the power of the spirit. And here I mean not just the Holy Spirit, but the spirit of character. He knew that men could be more than the sum of their parts because that was his experience. He had worked himself up, with help from his good luck charm called Paula, from most humble beginnings to celebrity status of sorts. He would try throughout his life and coaching career to instill that same sense of power—the ability to go beyond oneself—into all of his players, and into us, his daughters. To that end he would plaster the locker room and his office with motivational sayings. He would have them printed on large rectangular pieces of paper that he would have laminated. He would then stick them to the walls. Some of his favorites were:

"There will always be rocks in the road ahead of us. They will be stumbling blocks or stepping stones; it depends on how you use them."

Friedrich Nietzsche

"Excellence is an art won by training and habituation. We do not act rightly because we have virtue or excellence, but we rather have those because we acted rightly. We are what we do repeatedly. Excellence, therefore, is not an act but a habit."

Aristotle

"*The will to win, the desire to succeed, the urge to reach your full potential…these are the keys that will unlock the door to personal excellence.*"

Confucius

"*The difficult is done at once, the impossible takes a little longer.*"

English proverb

"*He who lives without discipline, lives without honor.*"

Icelandic proverb

"*Fortune favors the bold.*"

English proverb

"*All things are difficult before they are easy.*"

Chinese proverb

"*If you work hard enough at it you can even grind an iron rod down to a needle.*"

Chinese proverb

"*The reputation of a thousand years may be determined by the conduct of one hour.*"

English proverb

"If you can't get enthusiastic about your work, it's time to get alarmed—something is wrong. Compete with yourself. Set your teeth and dive into the job of breaking your own record. No one keeps enthusiasm automatically. Enthusiasm must be nourished with new actions, new aspirations, new efforts, new vision. It's one's own fault if enthusiasm is gone; he has failed to feed it. If you want to turn hours into minutes renew your enthusiasm."

Old Egyptian Historical Papers

"Our greatest glory consists not in never falling, but in rising every time we fail."

American proverb

By second grade, my sister and I could write sufficiently well enough that Daddy would pay us a nickel for each quote we wrote. In the early days, this was a task we loved, because once again it was special time with Daddy, with the added bonus of getting paid for it. By the time my father was moving through the college coaching ranks our pay had risen to a quarter, and then a dollar. But, once the teenage years set in, regardless of the pay, the opportunity cost of spending time with Daddy became too high.

In the 1980s, when Daddy was coaching for the New York Giants, the local press did a number of stories about my father. In one, some of his players were interviewed and they referenced his plastering of motivational quotes around the locker room. You might think that grown men would be immune to such hokiness, but for some, it left an impression.

By the time we left Richmond, I too, was developing a signature style which I felt left an impression; what today might be called an eclectic style. It all started in third grade, with white go-go boots. I spotted the boots in the window of a shoe store at the mall and nothing would do but to have them. I begged and begged my mother until she finally gave in. They were white leather, quite possibly fake for all I know or cared, of mid-calf height with a low heel. I wore those boots every single day and felt like I was hot stuff in them. My best look included colorful fishnet hose. The confidence I was feeling in my fashion sense was confirmed by the fact that on Valentine's Day, Damien, a classmate who was half my size with a crooked arm, asked me to be his. Q.E.D. (loosely translated as, so it is proven) as we say in the proof business!

CHAPTER 7

Rambling Wrecks from Georgia Tech;

and then there were three

> *"There is no limit to looking upward."*
>
> Japanese proverb

> *"I am thankful to all of those who said no. It's because of them I did it myself."*
>
> Albert Einstein

> *"If you are going nowhere, that's exactly where you will end up."*
>
> English proverb

I n the spring of 1967, Daddy got a job coaching at Georgia Tech in Atlanta, Georgia. This was an upward move, since Georgia Tech was a large school with plenty of resources, and a football tradition created on the back of Bobby Dodd, another UT graduate. The Georgia Tech staff ended up being a staff that contributed in a major way to the coaching ranks of the NFL for decades. Many from that time and place spun out like shooting stars across the league. The staff included Bud Carson, the head coach, one of my dad's best lifetime friends, and the guy responsible for the Steeler's Steel Curtain defense, which he devised with tutelage from my father; Gerry Glanville, most notably the Head Coach for the Houston Oilers and the Atlanta Falcons; and Tom Moore, who currently coaches the Arizona Cardinals, but also spent time with the Steelers, Lions, and Colts. So we packed a U-Haul one more time, and headed to Atlanta.

Until Daddy could settle in and we could find a new house closer to Atlanta, we girls and Momma spent the first two months in Cartersville in Southern hell. Every day to school I would wear my white go-go boots with different colors of fishnet hose, depending on my dress choice. My favorite ensemble was an orange, yellow, and purple striped dress, purple fishnets, and the white go-go boots. With accessories such as mine, I knew I was the wildest, spunkiest thing to come to Cartersville since my daddy left town. This was confirmed one day when one of my black classmates said, "You sure are colorful for a white girl." I was proud as I could be. I was also consoled by the fact that my time there was only temporary.

In the Atlanta years, Daddy's style was developing, just like mine. He was introduced to sans-a-belt pants first. He was mad about them when they first came out, for they were almost as comfortable as his coaching pants. In addition, the slim fit helped accent his powerful upper body. In the last two years we lived in Atlanta, he could be seen wearing a polyester, lime green leisure suit that he had custom made, due to the disparity between the size and bulk of the top half of his body and that of his lower half. Underneath the jacket he would be wearing a slippery, wildly patterned shirt. If he had overheated, his clothes would have spontaneously fused to his body.

In the late spring of 1967, we moved into a split level house on a nice suburban street in Sandy Springs, Georgia, a suburb of Atlanta. We also got to go to a new school. I was finishing fourth grade by this time and Lisa, fifth. Momma got a job teaching special education in the same school district, but at a different school. We all knew we had reached the big time and were now solidly middle class.

I remember everything about that house. I got the larger bedroom on this move due to a rare compromise with Lisa. I chose to paint it purple. I grew to hate that color over the four years we lived there, and only returned to it in my adulthood. My favorite spot was the built-in shelving at the back of the garage. It was set up so that I had a comfortable place to sit on the long, waist-high shelf. The two taller shelves forming the L shape were fourteen inches apart so that they made the perfect first and second floor of my Barbie house. At the corner of the L was a ground-level window to the backyard, which I opened so that I could pull Barbie's car around back, and she could come and go to work or shopping that way.

I just loved playing with Barbie there, could do it for hours by myself, and did do it for years. I would dress and undress her for all of her work and shopping activities. I would marvel at her waist and boobs, not knowing that her lack of ribs is what gave her that impossible figure. I was amazed by, and would fret over, her impractical feet—the shape of which meant that she was always losing one shoe or another. I would worry about her calves cramping from all that tiptoe action. Ken or Cricket would drop by to spice things up every once in awhile, but for the most part, Barbie was happy in her solitary world. When she got bored, we would redecorate. "I think it's time to rearrange the living room," Barbie would say. Or, "That bedspread is looking ratty, I think it's time to go shopping for a new one." And she would jump in her car and zoom off to the mall.

I enjoyed designing and building Barbie's house and its contents the most. I used Legos to build her furniture, plus whatever found objects did the trick. A spool of thread was a footstool for her weary feet. A fabric remnant was her bedspread, and an overturned shoe box her bed. I would fall asleep at night thinking up new ways to arrange that living space, and dreaming of new things that I could build that would be cool, and that Barbie was sure to like.

Moving into your adolescence with Barbie as your role model, with an older sister who is prettier, with friends who are skinny when you are not, and in a household focused on physicality and excellence will make you question yourself, no matter how sure you are of your fashion sense. One evening, I was spending the night with one of my skinny girlfriends and we were getting ready for bed. As we undressed, I noticed the hard angles of my friend's hip bones; I ran my hands over the velvety round curves of my own hips flowing smoothly into my belly, sure that I was not made out of the same basic parts. I asked my friend if I could touch her hips. The feel of her dense bones and concavity of her stomach convinced me that I simply did not possess the same anatomy.

Similarly, my comparisons of my body to Lisa's left me feeling oafish and inadequate. I was short and she was tall. I was plump, round, even fat, depending on your point of view. She was lean. I had bright red hair, hers was auburn. I wore glasses and she did not. By sixth grade, people I knew would regularly tell me how beautiful my sister was. I took these pronouncements as evidence that I was not; that I needed to cultivate something else. Eventually, that something else became my mind, and later, my art.

During this period I tipped the scales at one hundred and fifty pounds. My mother grew so alarmed at the weight that I was gaining that she made me weigh myself in front of her. She promptly put me on a diet saying, "Lori, you need to lose at least twenty pounds to be healthy and fit. I'm going to work with you to do that, but you're going to have to give up Cheez-Its and Cokes." Over the course of a year I went from 150 plus pounds to under 120 pounds.

During the dieting period, I was sitting at my makeup mirror one day applying eyebrow pencil in that bright, white light when Lisa walked in. "You look pretty good from behind," she said. I sat up a bit straighter, but was unsure whether I should feel proud, or, if I had just been insulted. I did not respond. My mother told me I had beautiful legs. Over time hip bones began to emerge. My dad quit asking me how much weight I had lost when I got sick with the flu or a stomach virus.

...

My best friend for the four years we lived in Sandy Springs was Melrose, a girl my age who lived up the street. She was a small, wiry girl with pale, white skin, shoulder length, stringy brown hair, and large brown eyes. She was the youngest sister in a four-girl family of much older girls. Melrose was a precocious tomboy—she knew many things that I did not. She was a girl who never, and I mean never, played with Barbie! She was powerful, and canny in the ways of the world. I could sure use some of what she had.

We walked to and from school together playing kick the can. We snuck out together at night and smoked our first cigarettes. We learned about pot from her older sisters, although we never smoked it. We hung out together at the local bowling alley. We ordered Vietnam vet bracelets together and ceremoniously put them on each other. By seventh grade we were sharing our stories of making out under the bleachers at the high school football game. We were Girl Scouts together.

Scouting was a thing that kept us occupied after school and supposedly taught us how to be crafty and independent. For Melrose, Sandy, my other best friend from that period, and myself, scouting became a contest to earn badges. To earn a badge in scouting you have a list of assignments you have to complete, and typically a few things you have to make. For example, if you wanted to earn the sewing badge, which I did, you had to first sew a few buttons on a shirt, next you had to make a tube skirt and put elastic into the waistband. After that you had to go the fabric store, buy a pattern and make a dress. You might also have to darn a sock or cross stitch a doodad. Your mother would verify all of your efforts by initialing the dates of your accomplishments in your badge guide, which you turned in to your Scout Master. You would then wait for the badge to arrive. When it did, you would be awarded the badge in front of the troop so that you could walk up to the front of the room and take a victory lap of sorts. You would go home and immediately sew it on your sash. The object of the competition was to get badges covering all the front and climbing up the back of your sash—the look was totally cool. I achieved this feat, although not by much.

Scouting also involved some camping. As I mentioned earlier, I was not a camper, nor was anyone in my family, but when you are twelve, it can be an adventure. What turned out to be the culmination of our scouting experience was our sixth grade senior camping trip. As seniors Sandy, Melrose, myself, and the rest of the older girls, shared one big tent. It was one of those with a wooden floor and exterior flaps tied to stakes above the pitched roof.

On the first day we headed down to the creek to collect firewood. Accompanying us on this outing was the Scout Master's young son. Upon approaching the creek someone in the group pointed out how refreshing the water was and the fact that the little waterfall right there made a wonderful swimming hole. To this day I do not recall who went first—probably Melrose—but, the end result was that all of us ended up skinny dipping in that creek. The water was cold and bracing. It was swirling around the rocks, pooling in places, and swiftly moving on in others. We splashed around, sat on the rocks, floated with the currents, and engaged in mindless chatter.

Well, you know how time flies when you are having fun—so it was for us. After an hour or two, the Scout Master sent out patrols to look for us. Unfortunately, she stumbled upon us herself. She was most upset by the fact that her young son was with us, enjoying our frolic, and getting a good gander at the variety of budding breasts, and sprouting pubic hair. Our punishment was to be grounded in our tents.

You might think being grounded would be boring with no TV, radio, electric lights, and the like. But we girls knew how to make our own fun. Inspired by my roof adventures in Richmond, we decided to have a contest of flap sliding from the top of the pitch of the tent. Using bunk beds, we managed to climb to the center beam and pull ourselves outside of the tent and on to the roof. Once we mastered that move, we were off to the races. Our fun made some of the other girls jealous enough to rat us out. Our mothers were called, we were locked down for the rest of the camping trip, and in big trouble when we got home.

I can't speak for anyone else, but I got whipped with a flappy, leather sandal. My mom was embarrassed by, and angry at my behavior. "Lori, I expect more from you than this. You girls were totally uncivilized. Your behavior reflects poorly on this family, and I absolutely will not tolerate that. You're grounded for the next month."

My dad laughed at our antics in a way that seemed to signal his pride in our rebelliousness, saying, "I sure hope you enjoyed that dance, because now you've got to pay for it."

"I did," I said in my head. I knew if I said it out loud my dad was sure to pop me.

After that I lost interest in earning any more badges, which was a good thing, because the scouts also lost interest in me.

During this period my rock star ambitions peaked. Melrose's older sister had directed and starred in a high school musical production, which had left a huge impression on Melrose. When she told me about it afterwards, we decided that we would create one of our own. We arranged to sleep over that weekend at my house. She showed up with her stuffed pillow case, note pad, and flash light. That night we went to bed without any fuss, but not to sleep; we stayed up all night writing the scenes in a spiral notebook by the light of the flashlight. We picked music to match, rearranging our presentation, and brainstorming about who we would invite to be in our production. We included a number of Diana Ross and the Supremes songs, and fought over who would get to be Diana in each song.

We worked on this project for a good two months. We would practice in the open space in my living room on the aqua-colored shag carpet. We put that Supremes/Temptation album I bought with Grandpa Leachman on the stereo, and lip-synced the words to *I Second that Emotion* and *I'll Try Something New*. When we got to *Stop, In the Name of Love,* our competition really heated up.

"Melrose, you know I want to be Diana for this song."

"Lori, I look more like Diana, and anyways I'm better than you."

"You're just a white girl like me who can't sing either. And I have rhythm."

Weekly we took turns visiting the principal's office to plead our case to present our extravaganza. Every time he rejected it. The principal simply could not see the value in staging our vanity production.

...

During Daddy's first few years at Georgia Tech, the team struggled. Daddy, on more than one occasion, also struggled with his wild ways. In truth, everyone in coaching at the college level and above struggled to some degree with vice of one sort or another. Every team had a team physician who was known to give vitamin B shots in the locker room. The team doctor would regularly prescribe various forms of amphetamines and other medications for the staff, and also for the families, when asked. All of the energy enhancing substances were attempts to keep up with the rigorous physical demands of coaching during the Playing Season and Recruiting Season. Other medications were doled out for pain or infection.

Access to prescription drugs meant that the families seldom needed to see a doctor and, in my household at least, frequently self-diagnosed and medicated their ailments, and those of their children. Throughout my childhood, our family sore throat and cough home remedy was a combination of hot tea, whiskey, and honey. Later, when our third sister Lamara was born, paregoric would be the go-to solution when she was fussy or teething. If we had an infection, my mother would pop open a bottle of antibiotics on the kitchen tray or in the butter niche of the refrigerator, and treat us herself.

In the Atlanta years, a tray on the kitchen counter contained the pills my dad, mostly, would be taking. He experienced persistent back pain from his football injuries. He was also a complete believer in protein powder, niacin, a variety of B vitamins, glucosamine, and other 'natural' substances. He consumed these things like candy. They, in fact, became his candy, as he always loved sweets, especially hard candy that could be sucked on, but was preoccupied with maintaining his sculpted physical form. As the years passed, and my dad moved up in the coaching ranks, grew older and, as a consequence, dealt with more and constant pain, the tray morphed into one of the bottom two crisper drawers of my parent's refrigerator. As my mother said recently, "We both craved and loved relief. Today, if I don't get my meds on time, I will be crying like a baby."

Heavy drinking was also the norm in the football crowd, since these were the most manly of men. Everyone was always inviting coaches and staff to a party, or they were throwing one for themselves to release the pressure from the week, and/or celebrate the win, or mourn the loss, of the last game. The typical get together would take place at one of the coaches' homes. The kitchen or dining room table would become the bar. Liquor bottles, mixers, and cups would litter the top while a cooler would be strategically placed right under the lip of the table. It contained the beer and ice. I don't ever recall seeing any solid food at these events other than a few chips or peanuts.

As the evening would wear on, the crowd would begin to segregate by sex. The men would pitch back in the chairs around the table and tell recruiting stories, or replay the game.

"You know Pete, I just came back Friday from seeing the Blakley kid."

"Yeah, Lamar. I heard that kid's fast and agile."

"You bet he is. The kid has supple hips. But you know where I found him when I went to his school?"

"No idea."

"I met up with him as he was getting off of the dry cleaning truck. He was finishing his assignment in Dry Cleaning 101. Can you believe that?"

"I know you're not shittin' me because when I went to visit the kid from Tarboro last week, I met him in a pig pen. He was sloppin' the hogs. His class was Farming 105."

They would laugh, shake their heads in a disbelieving way, and lean back, balanced on the back two legs of the chairs as they took a long sip of beer, or whiskey.

The women would have congregated by then in the den or living room, comfortably settling themselves on the sofa, floor, or chairs. Their conversation would have veered into children, schedules, and/or fashion.

"Paula, I am really liking you as a blonde."

"Thanks Emily" mom would say as she smoothed her hair. "You know, I think Lamar prefers it as well."

"What are you planning on wearing to the fall banquet?" Emily would ask. "I think I am going to wear that navy blue dress I wore last year to the Christmas party. You know, the one with the V in the back."

"I loved that dress on you. I bet Dick can hardly keep his hands off of you in that." They would share a knowing look, and sly smile.

Given Daddy's early years, and the religious fervor exhibited by his mother, fear always trumped love with respect to the issue of God. This fact manifested in a number of healthy and not so healthy ways through the years, particularly given that he was a 'full tilt guy' as my mom liked to say. He would periodically give up everything—the pills, the alcohol, the smokes, the chewing tobacco, whatever altering or stimulating substances he was taking. He called these periods his 'purity regime.' It was Daddy's version of cleansing. He would go cold-turkey—with dedication. Sometimes the regime would last for months. For him, it was the equivalent of putting on a hair-shirt. It was his repentance and absolution.

While we admired his determination and commitment, these periods were always a bit stressful for everyone else. Daddy expected the entire household to be on his program. If we were not, we would be the recipient of a steady steam of commentary from him. "I see you're eating sweets again Lori. Do you think you need that?" Or, "Paula, what's that? Are you drinking another glass of wine? Don't you think you've had enough already?" Or, "Paula, are you smoking another cigarette? You just put one out a few minutes ago."

When his purity regime ended we were all always relieved because it meant he would no longer be monitoring everyone's consumption behavior. A blowout night of drinking, smoking, and carrying on with friends and/or fans would typically herald its demise.

...

When football season was over, the men came home. In our house, this was both good and bad. We loved and idolized our dad, but by this time, we knew that it was mom that made our lives run. Mom bought and sold the houses. Mom arranged the moving, and chose the schools. Mom paid the bills, and handled all of the money. Mom signed us up for dancing, and ran the carpool. So The Dude's efforts to establish his authority were a real bother.

"Lori, where're you going? Who'll be there? Who's picking you up? Who's chaperoning? You know you have to be home by 10."

"I'm going with Sandy, dad. Her mom's driving. You know Dude, when I went last month, mom let me stay until eleven."

"Well, I am not your mother, and I said be home at ten, and I mean it."

"You sure aren't," I whispered under my breath as I sulked away.

The domestication of Daddy during home time was also a challenge for him—a challenge that on more than one occasion was too much. It was early spring before Spring Training Season began, after Recruiting Season had ended, when Daddy had a colossal failure that played out in front of God and the entire neighborhood. My dad quite simply failed to come home.

In the hours before dawn my sister and I were awakened by the banging of the front screen door. We went to our bedroom windows, and lo and behold, if we did not see Momma hauling every one of dad's drawers, and all of his hanging things out into the front yard. Mom was dumping the drawers, and throwing his clothes all over the place, like the mad woman that she was. When the lawn looked like true white trash lived here, Momma lit up a cigarette and took a long drag. I could see her backlit figure standing at the outer edge of the reach of the porch light. Every time she would draw on that cigarette a thin light would illuminate the side of her face closest to me, and outline the hard set of her jaw. Once she had finished that smoke and was satisfied with her work, she turned on her heels, headed inside, and locked the front door.

Daddy came home as dawn was breaking and rushed up to the front door with a pile of clothes in his arms. Bang! Bang! Bang! His fists hit the door. Ding dong, ding dong, ding dong. He rang the bell over, and over, and over.

"Hot damnit Paula, let me in," he hissed through the door.

"Screw you, Lamar. Find some place else to land."

Of course no kid could sleep through all of this, especially after what we had already witnessed. We were watching through the bedroom windows. My dad scrambled frantically, in a herky jerky motion, to collect all of his clothes and stuff them into the trunk and back seat of his car. He then settled himself into the front seat, and went to sleep. When he woke up it was around 10 am. He again approached the front door.

Ding dong. "Girls! Come open the door and let me in." We silently did as asked.

Daddy moved quickly up the stairs and into their bedroom to confront Momma. The bedroom door slammed shut. Words and things flew between them. We could hear the occasional, "But Paula," "Horseshit," and bam! as something hit the wall or floor. After what seemed like hours of combat, my dad emerged like a chastised little boy. He sheepishly asked us to help him ferry his belongings from the car back into the house. We completed this task in total silence. You can bet that Lamar never made that mistake again.

...

By year three, the team was winning and going to bowls. The first bowl they ever went to was the Sun Bowl, which was located in El Paso, Texas. That was big stuff for Momma and Daddy. They left us with Grandma Leachman and flew off to a week-long party in the armpit of Texas. At the time my mother was pregnant with her third child.

Lamara Leigh was born that spring on March 7, 1971. This third child was my parents' last effort to have a boy. There was no discussion in our house about girl's names in the months leading up to the birth, because the male agenda was clear.

"I think we'll call him Robert, after your dad, but not a junior," mom suggested.

"I like the name Kevin," said Lisa.

"I like that OK, but I really like Geoffrey with a G," I chimed in.

Those were the days before ultrasounds, amniocentesis, and sophisticated blood tests. So when Lamara was born and my mother wanted to name her Lottie after her grandmother, my dad put his foot down.

"There's no way I am having a daughter named Lottie. It's an ugly, frumpy name, Paula."

My mother put her thinking cap on. She named her after Daddy. The way I see it, Lamara got the best name of the lot of us. However, as the third girl in our family, she was mostly ignored by Daddy.

Over time, all of us came to realize that the universe really does deliver to you what you should have, or need, or what is appropriate. Boys in our house would have been a lot of heartache and trauma. Any boy would have had to be perfect. He would have had to have been smart, play sports, and excel at all things. If he had been artistic or played the piano, those would have been fine attributes, but not ones my father could appreciate.

Being girls gave us a bit of leeway with respect to Daddy's expectations. But, living in a house filled with girls was a challenge for him. Except for appreciating our toughness and physicalness, and except for Paula, Daddy was not much into women. He simply did not understand women, or know how to talk to them. Until he had daughters, this was never a problem for him because women would always make the effort, and do the talking. At home his female audience was tougher. We wanted him to make the effort with us. When he did, his conversations focused on what we were doing or accomplishing. He was not the least bit interested in talking about what we were wearing, or reading, or feeling, or thinking. Cerebral things were not my father's focus. As for my mother, she was his lover, and his mate, and his teacher, and his coach. She filled a completely unique space in my dad's sexual schema; he both wanted and needed her.

...

Lamara's presence was a sea change for Lisa and me. We were now the young adults and the built in babysitters. I can't say we were especially good or loving at this task, since it was typically a contest of who could wait the other one out on the diaper change, or collecting the baby after nap time. When Lamara was about a year old, mother was out, and Lisa and I were in charge. I fed Lamara lunch, and left her playing in her high chair. After a time she began to cry.

"Lisa, I fed her. It's your turn to check," I yelled.

"Lori, I'm busy. If you're so worried about it, you do it."

"Lisaaaa! It's your turn!"

"Well, she'll just have to wait until I am good and ready."

The crying escalated until I finally could not take it. I walked around the corner of the kitchen and there was Lamara hanging by her fingernails, chin just above the highchair tray, covered in her own shit. I mean it was the loose, yellow kind that had greased her slide, covered her back, matted her hair, and stunk to high heavens. I claimed and cleaned the baby while Lisa looked on and laughed. She said, "You're the one who found it, so it's yours to clean up." I never forgave Lisa for that.

About this time, Lamara was learning to propel herself across a room by rolling. She had this peculiar habit of rocking her head side to side, twirling her hands in circles, and rolling everywhere. As I grew older, I realized that Lamara's particular combination of motor skills were her version of my thumb sucking. Everyone who has sucked their thumb, or knows someone who does or did, knows that there is always another 'tell' associated with the act—such things as rubbing your ear, rubbing the collar of your shirt, or T-shirt sleeve, or blanket, twirling or stroking your hair, or rubbing the outside of your pointer finger. It seems that self-soothing in all its forms takes coordination and focus.

Lamara was so sufficient in her self-soothing and motoring that she completely skipped the crawling stage. She reminded us of a loosey goosey bag of beans as she rolled around. So, Lisa and I began calling her Baby Beans. Eventually Momma modified Baby Beans into Miss Bea, and then simply Bea, the name we still use today.

...

During these Altanta years we took a family vacation to Jekyll Island, Georgia, and stayed in a very nice hotel right on the beach, with a pool and a golf course. We met a number of dad's Cartersville friends and their families there. Lisa and I were playing in the pool with some of those Cartersville kids when all of a sudden, they began leaping out of the water like penguins, grabbing their towels, and vacating the pool area. Lisa and I continued to splash around and play for a bit until we realized that we were the only two left from our group. We swam up to Momma, who was laying on the side in her baby blue two-piece and Jackie-O shades, reading a Harold Robbins novel.

"Mom, where'd all the other kids go? Why'd they leave?" we whispered.

"Girls, they got out when those black kids got in the water. They're just being ignorant. Forget about those Cartersville kids. That's their issue not ours. Just enjoy yourselves. Anyway, now you won't have to wait in line for the diving board."

Then and now, that is one of the moments that makes me most proud of my mother.

One of the others is my parents' mentoring of Bud, as well as a number of other young men. Mentoring, in fact, was what brought Daddy to Georgia Tech in the first place. In Savannah, he had coached a young man named Jack O'Neal. Jack came from a large Irish family, and, just like Daddy and Bud, football was Jack's ticket to college. He was a star high school quarterback, and was heavily recruited in the South. He chose Georgia Tech on the one condition that they hire my father to be his coach. So when my father first came to Tech, he was an offensive coach, but, at some point during those Georgia Tech years he moved to defense. It is most likely this duality that made him one of the best defensive minds of his generation. Such football greats as Lawrence Taylor and Leonard Marshall have paid tribute to his knowledge and teaching skills in their memoirs.

However, being a great coach and mentor will not necessarily save you from being fired in competitive football. In the last year that my father coached at Georgia Tech, the team played in the annual Peach Bowl in Atlanta, Georgia. Since the bowl was in our home town, Lisa and I got to attend. It was a miserable affair and the Yellow Jackets played miserably, in pouring down rain, on a sloppy field. We lost. Although the team had had a winning season, they were not winning in the way that was expected from Georgia Tech football; foreshadowing the importance of expectation, a lesson I was destined to learn later that year. Shortly thereafter and, to the surprise of the entire staff, we were fired. We were the first football coaching staff to be fired in the history of Georgia Tech football.

The event is seared in my memory because of the way we found out. One day I was lying in the living room on the floor listening to a country record on the stereo. The song that was playing was appropriately enough titled "Sink the Bismarck." The phone rang and I answered it.

"This is Tom Smith from the Atlanta Journal. My I speak to Lamar Leachman please?"

"Sorry, but he's not home right now. May I take a message?"

"Is this his daughter?"

"Yes it is."

"You know the entire coaching staff was let go this morning. How does it feel to be fired?"

I had no idea what he was talking about. "Moooooomm, pick up the phone!" I yelled.

This experience, more than any other in my childhood, taught me that although football was central to our lives, it was what my father did for a living. And, he loved it. But as a family, we couldn't afford to give our whole hearts to any one team the way fans do, because we would be moving to a new team and town shortly.

I had a friend at this time whose parents had an RV that they kept parked in their driveway to take to Athens, Georgia, for all of the University of Georgia home football games. They were dedicated fans. They painted their dining room red and black with 'Go Dawgs' in white lettering over the side board. They were expressing their support for the University of Georgia in the run up to its rivalry with Georgia Tech. When I first saw the room I thought, "They can only be so invested because the outcome of the game does not really affect the way they live." For my family, football was a razor's edge that could, and did, draw blood. Why would I do anything to give it a bigger role in our lives?

Over time, I came to realize that while my family and I felt the consequences of winning or losing any particular game, in any particular season, much more acutely than others, the fans possessed greater commitment, and sustained enthusiasm. Many of them did live for the game. They knew all the players by name and number, something that never would have occurred to me to bother with. They created family rituals around game day; we had our own, which never included my dad. They knew their versions of the ecstasy of winning and the agony of defeat; these experiences became ways to for them to bond and communicate.

We were different in other ways as well. Football determined the pulse of our daily lives. There was no nine to five regularity associated with work; it was all or nothing. There was no weekend break during football season. The weekend was the peak of the week in terms of pressure and performance. And, once my dad entered the ranks of professional coaching, there was no normal Thanksgiving or Christmas. It was the Playing Season.

CHAPTER 8

Tigers and Gamecocks

"A vision without action is a daydream. An action without vision is a nightmare."

Japanese proverb

"Victory belongs to the most persevering."

American proverb

"Morning is welcome to the industrious."

American proverb

Once again we packed up our possessions and moved. This time however, we had actual movers do the dirty work for us. We moved to Memphis, Tennessee, where my father had gotten a job as defensive coordinator for the Memphis State Tigers. There he coached with Fred Pancoast, who went on to be the longtime head coach at Vanderbilt, and Lindy Infante, who became another NFL coach. We bought an even bigger, nicer house in the Memphis suburbs next to a village called Germantown, where we were enrolled in high school.

Memphis is the place where it dawned on me that we actually had money to spare. This awareness was reinforced by the fact that when we started school that fall, my mother took Lisa and me to Casual Corner and told us we could buy three dresses apiece. I still remember my selections. One was a white flannel jumper that buttoned up the front with small blue and pink flowers, and alternating colored buttons. One had a full skirt. It was red with white polka dots on the skirt, and white with red poka dots on the bodice. The third was a floral, empire waist number, with a U neck and long sleeves.

By this time, I was was entering ninth grade and Lisa tenth, while Lamara was on the cusp of toddling. Lisa and I were at the beginning of a period where we would change high schools every year. I was still wearing glasses, and we were both in braces. Lisa was growing taller and leaner. I was short and more zaftig. I was jealous of Lisa and her physical beauty. However, I needed her and she needed me to weather the transitions, so we were evolving into frenemies.

The year was 1972. Across America bussing was being instituted as a partial solution to school segregation. The South generally, and Memphis specifically, were at the heart of that process. Since Germantown High School was the best public high school in the Memphis area, it was ground zero.

The bussing program meant that our school's buses started in the outlying, rural areas, where they picked up the black kids first. By the time they got to our neighborhood every seat on the bus was 'filled' with one young African American man or woman. As you boarded the bus you would have to ask, "Can I sit here? Can you move over a little?"

Some would say, "no," with, or without, looking at you. Others would raise their head, look you in the eye, and then place their head back in the crook of their arm which was resting on the seat back in front of them. They would not move one inch, or utter one word.

As you worked your way down the aisle of the bus, others would look you up and down slooooooowly, then ever so much more slowly move over two to three inches, grudgingly letting you perch yourself on the outer edge of the seat. It was most certainly their protest, and possibly their preemptive defense, but it also just sucked—making every school day start with a confrontation.

Once you got to school the routine of classes would begin. Between class changes, if you needed to use the restroom, you had to make long detours since there were, unofficially of course, restrooms that only the white kids used, and others that only the black kids used. If by chance you entered the wrong one, you knew in an instant, and backed out quickly, in case someone was coming in behind you. The cafeteria was equally self-segregated with white kids on one side, and blacks on the other. Pep rallies, which were designed to bring the school together in the spirit of friendly competition, were also characterized by self-imposed racial segregation.

The only integrated student bodies were the sports teams. Since winning was the number one priority of our high school teams, skin color did not matter much if you had talent and drive. Given that this was the year that Title IX was passed, the sport teams provided a mechanism for the boys to cross the racial divide much more easily than the girls.

The bus ride home featured its own racial parting of the seas. In the afternoon the entire racial geography of the bus changed. The black kids would own the back of the bus, and us white kids would take the seats at the front. You would think this back of the bus arrangement would be anathema to the black students, but they actually chose it, and enforced it. If you happened to be a white girl who was late to the bus so that all the front seats were taken, you would squeeze in as the third on a seat, to avoid breaking the invisible barrier separating front from back, white from black.

I learned some important things from this period in my life. Probably the most important with respect to race was that the anger of the parents was totally manifest in the children. While you might have an African American friend—and we did—she could like you and befriend you in isolation, but get her in a group or at home in the presence of her family, and you were persona non grata. You could just not overcome the collective anger of the times on either side of the racial divide. Nor could you cultivate peace and understanding by simply throwing groups with real differences together. Trust can only be cultivated through repeated positive interaction.

On the one occasion our friend Denise came to spend the night at our house, as the three of us exited the bus, one of the black kids said, "Girl, where you goin' with those crackers?" My mother was also clearly surprised when the three of us walked into the house and dropped our books on the kitchen table.

"You didn't tell me she was black," my mother said in private, after dinner.

"Didn't think of it, mom. Does it matter?"

"Not so much to me, but I'm not sure what her parents will think when they pick her up tomorrow."

This was a prescient observation. When Denise's mom pulled into the driveway the next day she was clearly agitated, and confused. She got out of her car slowly and hesitantly, just as we came out through the garage door to meet her.

"Get your things Denise. It's time to go," she said curtly.

"But don't you want to come in for a minute and meet Mrs. Leachman?"

"I don't have time, Denise. We need to go. Now!"

That next week at school we learned that Denise would never be spending the night with us again, and we would never be going home with her after school.

I recall thinking that when we moved to Memphis, I would adopt a new M.O. It would make me the cool person I always wanted to be. What I found was that I might adopt a cool mannerism or saying, but my essential self was set. I was straight-forward, earthy, and colorful. This is a very important lesson to learn early, especially when your family moves a lot. Otherwise you will twist in the social cross currents like a kite in the wind on blustery day. I am sure it is one of the reasons that many people find me uncompromising to this day.

A third critical lesson to come out of that time and place was that expectation and attitude are everything. When we moved to Memphis, I was determined to hate it. Making new friends in a high school that was fraught with divisions and tensions was a challenge. We had lived in Atlanta for four years, and I had loved it there. So, I made myself hate

Memphis for about the first six months. But, by the time we moved away six short months later, I had grown to appreciate the place and value new friends. I realized that I had wasted a good bit of time and misery on self pity when I could have been engaged in much more positive ways. I also became aware of the fact that change is good, but transition can be a bitch.

...

Lisa and I had taken ballet lessons from the time I was four and she was five. In Memphis, all those years of lessons resulted in us being asked to join the Memphis ballet. In truth, Lisa was asked to join and I was just along for the ride. I was no longer fat, but I was not professional ballet material. We spent many hours each week at the barre, learning to be loose in jazz, and cultivating rhythm and coordination in tap. We also cultivated some major eating disorders. This was the period where bulimic tendencies emerged—more strongly manifested in Lisa, since she had the real potential—and the abuse of laxatives. The little pink pill known as Correctol was a staple in our medicine cabinet. If you overate, you could either throw it up, or purge it out. One has to ask oneself what it says about a country when what is known as the 'little pink pill'—Addyi is too new to count—is a laxative used, and abused, almost exclusively by women, and what is know as the 'little blue pill' is a sexually enhancing drug used, and abused, by men.

After a particularly filling dinner, if we were at home, Lisa or I would frequently disappear upstairs about half an hour after we were done. One of us would emerge later with a satisfied look on our face and pop open a container of low-cal yogurt. This was a sure sign that the dinner that had gone down had come right back up.

During the year in Memphis, we were allowed to shop for our first pairs of blue jeans. It was the 1970s and Daddy had relaxed a bit on his couture standards, with some subtle urging from Momma. I brought my first pair of peanut bell bottoms; peanut because the zipper was so small, and bell bottoms because the legs were so large and full. They looked great on Lisa but were not my best look. My round belly bulged over the low rise of the waist band, and the full legs accentuated the narrowness of my hips. However, if Lisa had a pair, then I should too, and, as has been established, poor fashion choices had never stopped me in the past.

When I got those jeans home, I got busy. They were the perfect canvas for embroidering my zodiac sign and an assortment of rainbows, rays of sunshine, and musical notes. That sewing badge from my Girl Scout days was really paying off. A few weeks later, when I descended the stairs to go out for a family dinner, Daddy about had a heart attack.

"Where did you get those hippie pants?" he said, as he looked me up and down with pursed lips and squinty eyes.

"They're my new jeans. I just added a few things of my own. Aren't they cool?"

"They're hippie pants. You can't go out of the house with me in them. Go change."

"Are you kidding? These jeans were more expensive than the pants you have on."

"I don't care if they are made out of real gold lamé, you will not be wearing them with me. Go change."

"I just won't go then."

"Well, that's your choice, but if you're coming with me, it'll be dressed in somethin' different."

I stayed home.

While in Memphis, Lisa and I attended our first live concert. It was the BeeGees. We went with an older girl from down the street. Julie could drive, and so it was that we all set out for the concert, feeling truly independent, and grown up at last. I don't remember much about the concert or the music, which says something about the BeeGees and the white toast nature of the event. What does stick with me about the evening is the feeling I had setting out; three cool girls, with their own car, heading to a rock concert, in embroidered blue jeans.

There was a cute boy in our neighborhood named Stephen. He lived across the street. He had dark curly hair and a swarthy completion. None of us found Stephen attractive in a physical sense, because he was somewhat effeminate, and Lisa and I, being daughters of a football coach, were only interested in athletes by that time. Stephen did not play sports and did play the piano. He was always clean and organized in his appearance, and rarely sweaty. He was not a fast runner or adventuresome tree climber. However, Stephen made a great friend and taught us how to play Mah Jongg.

I loved that game. I loved the look and click of the tiles as they were being played or reshuffled. I loved the attention the game required, and the fact that it could last for days. In our family we rarely played board games or cards together. This had something to with the fact that what my dad did for a living was a game. Dad's occupation meant that if you were engaged in gaming of any sort there had to be more at stake than just the fun of the game. Winning, money, reputation were necessary to capture the time and interest of Lamar, and by extension, us.

...

Given our short time in Memphis, it was rather surprising all the new things that we were exposed to and all of the things that we learned. However, by the spring of 1973, Daddy had taken a job with the South Carolina Gamecocks (USC), and we headed back towards the east coast. We bought another nice suburban spread in the outer regions of Columbia, South Carolina. The little town was called Irmo: we were enrolled in, and attended, Irmo High School.

At USC, my father coached under Paul Dietzel, another one of those coaching dynasties in the Wally Butts and Bear Bryant vein, only less so. South Carolina was a clear step up since they had a private plane, and flew Daddy there in it for his interview.

"You know Paula, Paul is sending a private plane to pick me up for the interview. The school must have resources. I think I can work for him. The football tradition is certainly better. How do you feel about moving to Columbia?"

"Lamar, if the pay's right and it's easier to win there, I'm all for it. You know the girls and I can make a home anywhere. So you need to really assess the potential on your visit. We can discuss it when you get back."

Memphis was the place where critical life lessons were forged and Columbia was the place where Lisa and I gave up ballet, learned to drive, and tied on our first drunk. Abandoning ballet came first, since there was no real professional ballet organization in the area at the time. We both did try the local proxy, but it was run by a severe, pretentious woman, given the real lack of professional rigor, with hair down to her knees. We were fascinated by her hair, but lost interest in the lessons after a couple of months. The jettison was fueled by the offer of a horse from Momma if we gave up the lessons; she had always wanted a horse, as it turns out. We traded in our toe shoes for stirrups, and Momma bought an American Standard horse by the name of Tom Grey. She did not tell Daddy, and she swore us to secrecy.

We boarded him across the street from the high school and rode him most afternoons. Outside of being the daughters of the new college football coach, our cachet was further elevated by the five feet you could gain sitting on the back of that horse. We would take turns riding him on the shoulder of the main road and down to the football practice fields, so all the boys could appreciate how well we sat a saddle. The height and the speed of that galloping horse provided a new means of achieving that flying sensation.

Frequently, Daddy would be coming home from work, car pooling with three other coaches who called Irmo home, when they would see either Lisa or me galloping down the road on Tom. Daddy was always impressed and amazed at this, and would say to the car, "Would you look at that. I have no idea where my girls learned how to ride like that, or where they rent that horse." It was all that car full of men could do to keep from busting out laughing. My father was the only one of them who did not know that we—he—owned that horse!

Daddy was on a strictly need-to-know basis with respect to pretty much everything but sport. Certainly all issues on the home front were strained through the Paula filter. Since Momma handled all things domestic and financial, the horse was a secret that was easy to keep. No matter what Momma brought home, she never told you honestly what she paid for it. I only know the true price of the dining room set she acquired in Richmond because I was there. Mother never bothered Daddy with financial details, our educational issues, or her, or our, social schedules. She also used the need-to-know criteria, combined with some modification of the full story, when informing Daddy of our youthful indiscretions. We all appreciated that, especially as the severity of our transgressions escalated.

One of the transgressions was drinking—which logically followed after driving. Learning to drive, as all of you know, is one complex affair. It requires concentration, a sense of place and space, as well as coordination. Factor a clutch into the mix and it is a most challenging task. Fortunately, Lisa had to master the challenge before I did. She also had a lot more trouble. Or, quite possibility, I had the benefit of learning from her mistakes.

One of the biggest laughs I ever shared with Momma came at Lisa's expense, making it much sweeter for me at the time. Lisa was learning to drive a Volkswagon. She was taking the car to visit a girlfriend. She had her learner's permit, which allowed her to drive during the day, at fifteen, without an adult in the car. She got the car into reverse and rolled it out of the driveway. Once in the street, she had to get it into first gear and ease off the clutch for lift off. Every time she tried, the car stalled out like a buckin' bronco.

Now Lisa has always had long, thick, beautiful auburn hair, and on this particular day she was wearing it in a pony tail on the top of her head. Every time that car stalled out her head would jerk around like one of those spring loaded bobble heads you find on the rear dashboard of cars in the South. Her ponytail would be sent a bobbin' and twirlin' like the pasties on a stripper's boobs.

I came upon Momma watching this from a front window laughing, with tears streaming down her face. "Lori, you've got to see this. Lisa has been out there for ten minutes and can't get the car out of first gear. Here, sit on the floor so she can't see us in the window." We both were laughing so hard we were crying, while Lisa was out there cussin', bobbin,' and twirlin.' I thought, "Surely she will come in and ask for help." But no, not Lisa, which tells you something about her will and pride, and my parents' lasting influence. After about thirty minutes of effort, she squealed out of there, burning rubber, never looking back. We did not speak of the incident until Lisa was well past thirty.

Since we could drive during the day without an adult, Daddy had no problem with us driving at night under the same conditions. He stated simply, "If I didn't think you could drive, I would not let you behind the wheel. Period!" This fact further elevated our status among our peers.

One night, Lisa was driving a group of us girls to the high school football game and then to the local Pizza Hut, where our clique liked to congregate after the game. Someone in our group had procured a couple of bottles of Boone's Farm wine. So, periodically we would stroll out to the car for a nip. Not being the seasoned drinker that I am now, the next thing I knew, I was draped across the back seat of that Volkswagon throwing up out of one back door, feet dangling out of the other. It was not my finest moment. That experience has left me with a longstanding sensitivity to, and revulsion for, the smell of sweet wines.

Years later, when Daddy was coaching for Toronto, a British couple became good family friends. They introduced us to such delicacies as beans on toast, and we introduced them to grits and boiled peanuts. They educated us on the finer points of rugby, and we provided them with an up close and personal look at western football. You might say it was a high order cultural exchange.

One of the things that Sally and Stewart also introduced me to was a whiskey sour. It was a game day, and they were coming with us. To get prepped for the day, I dropped by their place for brunch. It was a special menu of beans on toast—this also included an egg in the center for those of you who are unfamiliar with the British specialty—and whiskey sours, since this was Sally's favorite drink at the time. I want you to pause here and really think about that dining combination... After brunch, I continued to drink those babies like water throughout the day, since the stadium had a private club for family and friends of the team. By the time we got home from the game that evening, I was sick as a dog. To this day, all I recall of the incident is a whole lot of whiteness, the feel of the cold bathroom floor tile against my side, and the smell of whiskey sours. Just a whiff of that smell still makes me gag.

Later that fall, on another Friday night, my best friend Anne, the third girl in our circle Donna Rice, and I headed over to the local Pizza Hut as usual for our post-game hanging out and drinking. Donna was the beautiful girl in our circle. Anne was the sexy girl; men and boys were drawn to her like moths to a flame. I was what? The red-headed girl; the coach's daughter; the girl with the horse; the new girl. I was the girl who had learned her lesson regarding Boone's Farm wine. I stuck to cokes, as did Donna. Anne was the one who over indulged. When we arrived back at my house later that night, she was slurring and bobbing.

"Loooori, I think I am going to be sick," she choked out as she was beginning to heave.

I rushed her quickly into the bathroom and held her hair back as she threw up in, as well as around, the toilet. "Anne, I'm going to lean you against the sink. I don't want you to move while I clean this up. You might fall or break something."

Just as I was placing the last towel in the bottom of the hamper Anne pushed away from the counter in an effort to leave the bathroom. As she did she swerved, tilted, grabbed the floral patterned shower curtain, and fell like an upturned beetle into the tub. The shower curtain came crashing down, curtain rings clanging against the rod and tiles. I quickly forced the curtain and rod back into position, and yanked Anne up and out of the tub. She made such a racket that Daddy popped in to check on us. Such was his faith in our innocence as young Southern girls that he had no clue anything was amiss.

Or so I thought, until the next morning. Bam! Bam! Bam! It was seven a.m. and my daddy was pounding on my bedroom door. "Lori! Anne! time to get up. You have work to do."

"Go away daddy. It is only seven o'clock, and it's Saturday."

"I know what day and time it is—we're playing Florida State today and I am heading into the office shortly. Get your butts out of bed. You have work to do. I want to show you what I expect from you."

"Are you kidding? It's the weekend and we're tired."

"I bet you are. Now get your butts out of bed and be in the kitchen in five minutes, or I'll be in there and drag you out."

He had an urgent task that involved yard work that absolutely had to be completed that morning. It required both of us to dedicate the next several hours to hard labor. It was all Anne could do to hold the rake and move through the motions required to move earth and plant material around, organize it, and dispose of it. She had to break frequently during our toil, leaving me to shoulder the bulk of the burden of our assignment. When she did take a break, she splayed herself across the edge of the patio, and the sunlight caught her pasty, sweaty skin. What is clear from this incident is that my father was no fool, and while his mechanisms for motivation were mostly mental, his mechanisms for discipline were always physical.

...

During these early high school years, Lisa and I became interested in attending practice, meeting dad for lunch in the dining hall, and/or filling in in the coaching office if the secretaries needed someone to answer the phone. All of these efforts were really attempts to check out the boys, his players, and strut whatever stuff we thought we had.

On the practice field, Daddy was always the loudest, most animated guy out there. We could tell that he just loved the game and everything about it. His enthusiasm infected us. His behavior made us proud, and a bit jealous. He was constantly heckling, joking, and praising his players.

"Hollywood, you should be wearing a dress today the way you're playing. Are you afraid of breaking a nail? Messin' up your hair?"

"Hec, you must have done some sinnin' last night. You're sure moving slow. Repent now boy and get the job done."

"Depo, way to go darling.' Now, get up and do it again, but this time, be quicker off the line."

"Get-em, get-em, get-em, boys! I'm the law, and I'm after you."

In the cafeteria line the banter was constant.

"Coach, I see you are with the ladies today. Girls, what are you doing with this guy? You know he's a scoundrel."

"Hec, I'll see you in the weight room later and be adding another twenty pounds to your bench press. These ladies are my girls."

"Coach, with that ugly mug, how'd you end up with daughters like these?"

"The key is to marry well, son. You can only hope."

And so it would go as we pushed our trays through the line, and settled into a table by the window with other coaches or staff.

CHAPTER 9

Crossing the
Mason-Dixon Line

"Only a person who risks is free."

Unknown proverb

"First deserve it, then desire it."

American proverb

"You can't wait for inspiration. You have to go after it with a club."

Jack London

In the spring of 1974, Daddy got a job coaching professional ball for the New York Stars in the World Football League (WFL). We packed up our gear and headed north for the first time in our lives. Daddy went on ahead to get the ball rolling, so to speak, and Momma packed us three girls, our dog, a large Irish Setter, and her favorite house plants into an old brown station wagon for our pilgrimage north, having traded in the Volkswagon for something safer. We looked like white trash spilling like we were from every opening in that car. As we came across the Verrazano Bridge, our eyes were popping from the view of the New York skyline. We looked down below the bridge and saw kids playing in the street in the water from a broken fire hydrant. Traffic slowed to a crawl, and we got a long, slow view of the densely packed cemetery that fronts the expressway leading out to Long Island. It was a snapshot of every stereotype we had ever had of New York City.

If you are wondering what in the world the WFL was, you are probably not alone. In 1973, a group of investors came together in an attempt to establish a second professional football league to compete with the NFL. The ultimate goal was to establish a truly global American style football league. To that end, the first franchises were sold to investors across the U.S. Most of the teams where located in the South, since that is where the absence of American professional teams was most pronounced. However, the league knew it would not be taken seriously without a franchise in the New York City area.

The New York Stars started as a Boston franchise. However, the financial backing could not be solidified, so the team was sold to Bob Schmertz, and moved to New York City. The head coach was a guy named Babe Parilli who had played for the Jets during their storied victory in Super Bowl III. The team and the league were a composition of former NFL players, semi-pro recruits, and rookies.

When we first arrived in New York, the team was in the middle of Pre-season camp. For every professional team this is akin to sifting the wheat from the chaff, leavening the bread, and letting the jello solidify. Coaches work from seven a.m. to twelve p.m. every day. They take all of their meals with the team, and frequently spend the night at camp, depending on the location. The players practice two times a day, and each practice is filmed. Coaches spend the evening hours reviewing the films and grading the players' reaction times, ability to read the plays, aggressiveness, and the like. Whoever does not make the grade is cut, until the team converges on its playing roster by the end of the pre-season games.

For a tight team, training camp is like being at boys camp. For the wives and families it is much less fun. On this move, the families were all living in student dorms, with the bulk of our personal possessions in storage, and with little room to move around in. Our dorm living meant that Lisa and I had no opportunity to meet kids our own age. So, for Lisa and me it was a summer of romance novels and fighting. On occasion, our boredom was broken by excursions to the beach, or playing tennis. Then we had our first trip ever into Manhattan.

Marilyn, one of the coaches' wives, grew up in the area. She saw our frustration and took pity on us by arranging a day for both of us in the city. I do not remember where we went first, but we ended our day with a walk through Greenwich Village, followed by dinner in a charming Italian restaurant. The restaurant had an enclosed courtyard in the back where we sat under twinkling strings of white lights while eating an authentic Italian meal. But the thing that really preoccupied me was what I had just seen. Walking the streets of the Village in the mid 1970s at dusk completely blew my mind. For the first time in my life, I saw homosexuals, lesbians, cross dressers, and transvestites. I could not tell who was female, or male. In my family, maleness was as tangible as the shirt I was wearing. The scene rocked my world.

"Lisa, do you see that?" I whispered as we passed a young man? woman? in sparkling platform shoes, bell bottoms, and a T shirt, with big hair and nail polish.

"Sure do. Are those guys holding hands?"

"Looks like it. Do you think the person in the platform shoes is male or female?"

"Not sure, but I think it's a guy."

I was not the only one whose sense of sexuality was broadened that summer. My dad and some of his coaching compatriots also got a few sex education lessons. To break the monotony of camp and have a change of scenery, a group of the coaches and their wives arranged an excursion to Fire Island one Saturday. They had heard that the Island had an outrageous party scene, and they knew they had always been guys who were the life of a party.

To hear them tell it, for they did retell it many times in the days after, and the years to come, as soon as they boarded the ferry they knew something was different. And no, they did not know that Fire Island was the Mecca of gay culture in the summer. As I have said, my father had an upper body that women loved and men admired. That body made him the object of desire for most of the men on this particular boat. He was used to being admired and envied, but this kind of attention was something that he had never experienced. The overt sexual interest from other men made him proud in a most uncomfortable way and, slightly embarrassed. Once they got to the island, the blatant sexuality of the homosexual partygoers made my dad and his friends nervous, and more than a little appreciative that they were accompanied by their wives—anybody could see that they were clearly heterosexual.

For weeks after this excursion, we would hear Daddy describing the scene with a weird, embarrassed grin on his face, accompanied by an uneasy laugh. The small town boy from Catersville in him was working on coming to terms with the sexual revolution.

"Paula, the night we went to Fire Island, did you see those four guys in dresses? What was that about?" he asked one evening as he was cleaning and trimming his nails at the kitchen table.

Mom turned from the sink where she was just finishing up loading the dishwasher, "I think they're what you would call cross-dressers, Lamar."

He looked up from his task with a furrowed brow, squinted eyes, and firmly set mouth, "What's that mean? I thought they were all homos. Why'd a guy want to wear a dress?"

"I can't answer that, Lamar," she said, as she leaned back against the counter and crossed her arms over her chest. "Maybe he wants to pass for a woman. Or, maybe, he is the woman in the relationship."

Over time Daddy developed a radar for anything outside of the norms of traditional heterosexual sexuality. He was a macho, classically heterosexual guy from small town Georgia raised in the 1940s and 1950s. He was brought up in an atmosphere of religious fervor. These elements swirled around in him, stewed through the years as his experiences mounted, and resulted in a sixth sense for sexual differences of any type.

...

By the end of the summer we bought a house in Sayville, Long Island, and Lisa and I were enrolled in the local high school. Lisa was entering twelfth grade and I was entering eleventh. The only thing I remember about that high school is the first day. At lunch time, Lisa and I approached a table in the cafeteria and put our trays down. When we did, every person at the table got up and moved. As if they had choreographed it, one chair after another pushed back from the table, the occupant rose, picked up her lunch tray, then moved across the isle to another table. They executed a fan wave as they shunned us. Immediately we had the same thought: so this must be what it is like to be black in America.

When we drove home from school that day we sat in the driveway in my dad's black muscle car and cried. In that school they had not had a new student in years. My sister and I, with our red hair and Southern drawl, stood out as bothersome Southern interlopers.

However, I did make one very good friend. Loretta came from a large Irish family and was red-headed and freckled like me. She had a round, moon-pie face. Loretta loved dogs and hated cats. She had been terrified as a young child by the howling and carrying on of a pair of mating felines. Any loud meow or mewing would make her shudder and cover her ears. I spent the night with her often, and we would walk from her house to the jetty where all the kids hung out, and drank beer. She taught me how to bumper ride a car in the snow, but I was never very good at it, because I was just too afraid.

It was also during our time in Sayville that Lisa, being the boy magnet type, had her first serious boyfriend Bubba—if I'm lyin,' I'm dyin.' He was, of course, the star football player from the high school. Bubba was taller and bigger than my dad with brown hair and a Fu Manchu mustache. He dressed in flannel and blue jeans, and drove a truck. He had also recently broken up with the head cheerleader, which further cemented our status as pariahs at our new school.

Bubba was another young man that my father took under his wing in an effort to help him acquire a college education. Momma could see that Lisa was more than a little serious about him, so she nudged my dad into helping. Daddy brought Bubba to the attention of a number of college coaches. These efforts resulted in Bubba securing a football scholarship to university. However, Bubba had never been off of Long Island. His attachment to place ultimately lead him to turn down the scholarship and become a clammer like his dad. That decision played a meaningful role in the demise of his relationship with Lisa. Such was the insular mindset of our Sayville classmates.

...

On Saturdays that fall, we would pack up the car and carpool with the other coaches' wives and families to Randall's Island, where the team played their games in Downing Stadium. The location was scary and inaccessible—you could not get there by public transport, or without driving through Queens, a violent place back then. We had been informed by the team office manager, "If something rams your car, just keep driving. It's an attempt to get you out of your car. If you do stop and get out, you'll get robbed." No one had a cell phone back then, so this information simply served to heighten our sense of unease, and ensure that we traveled to and from the games in a convoy.

Playing at Downing Stadium was the kiss of death for the New York Stars. The stadium was poor by any standards. On a good night the lights would work, illuminating about half of the field. The turf was beat up brown grass. The conditions were so low rent that the team had to make a change. So, midway through the Stars' first season, the team was sold again, this time to a Charlotte investor, and moved to Charlotte, North Carolina. That franchise was renamed the Charlotte Hornets.

By this time, the Stars/Hornets were winning games, but the league was in financial trouble, and serious doubts were circulating about whether it would make it. Paychecks were not being issued, and bills were not being paid. For these reasons we did not move to Charlotte with the team. The coaches stayed in an extended-stay hotel during the remainder of the season, and commuted home to New York on an off week.

For my family this was a dire situation, since we were not rich and had two children on the brink of college. My parents depleted all of the money they had saved for Lisa's and my college expenses during this period. They also accumulated some serious debt. Our debt burden was compounded by the fact that a number of the team creditors sued individual coaches to recover some of their loses. My family was a victim of this strategy.

At the end of the season, Daddy and two other coaching colleagues would head up to a phone booth on the Montauk Highway to make phone calls about jobs. In college and professional coaching there was no process for hiring that involved sending out résumés with cover letters and the like. The entire system was based on contacts, word of mouth, your win-loss record, who and where you coached. This system continues today.

The men would take turns in the booth using a credit card billed to the team. The other two guys would sit in the relative warmth of the car talking football, and sharing contacts and information.

"I just heard from Jerry that there's an opening at University of Georgia for a quarterback coach. Are you interested, Tom?"

"Hell, Lamar, I don't know about you, but I'm interested in anything. Who's the right contact?"

"I think Bill Clay's your man. Do you know him?"

They would then head down to the unemployment office to collect a check. For my dad it was one of the most humbling times of his life, and for my family, it set us back financially for years.

The entire league folded in 1975.

Caption: Super Bowl winning defensive line

PART III

The Playing Season

This is the top season in football and happens in the fall. This is the season where lessons are learned, romances are formed, and hearts are broken; not necessarily in that order. This is the season when competition is king, when winning is everything.

CHAPTER 10

Crossing the Border

"Attitude is a little thing that makes a big difference."
Winston Churchill

"A small man can cast a large shadow."
English proverb

"No matter how hard the past, you can always begin again."
Buddhist proverb

I n the spring of 1975, Daddy got a job as defensive coordinator for the Toronto Argonauts, coaching under a head coach named Russ Jackson. Russ had been a star professional player in the CFL. Momma and Lamara made a quick exit from Long Island at the end of February, and joined Daddy in Toronto.

My parents wanted both Lisa and me to graduate from an American school since they were not sure about the Canadian system, or how it would translate for American universities. Momma did not have the time to research all of the dimensions regarding the education situation, visa and moving issues were more pressing. So Lisa and I headed back to Columbia, South Carolina, to live with friends, and finish high school in the U.S.

I went to live with Anne and her family, and Lisa went to live with her friend Kate and hers. I spent three full months with Anne and her family and they were wonderful to me. They treated me just like they did Anne. Given that her mother was a devout Christian and an upstanding member of the First Baptist Church, I became a regular attendee. Anne and I used the cover of our church youth group to flirt and carry on with boys, and the Sunday service to dress to impress them. Unlike us, these boys went to private school. They took us to our Junior/Senior Prom in a limo.

In truth, I really enjoyed that church and loved the choir music. It would roll up and over the congregation, and fill the space around you. The church had a large, elegant sanctuary with balconies on three sides. If I placed myself strategically in the balcony, I could eyeball all the coming and goings of the congregants, watch the passing of notes and pens up or down a row, and enjoy the pervasive fidgeting of the masses below me. Many a time I thought, "This must be what God sees when he's watching over us."

Meanwhile, Lisa was living with one of the most laid back and largest families I have ever seen. Here, I do not mean large in numbers, I mean large in size. Kate herself was a tall, large hipped girl with a beautiful smile. She, along with a younger brother Tiny, were the small ones in her family, and both of them were over six feet tall. Her mother, father, and sister were obese. Put the three of them in a room together and there was no room for anything else. Whenever I came over to visit, they would be cranked back in their loungers in their den watching TV. It did not take me long to figure out that recliners were critical equipment for people their size because they facilitated the change of position from sitting to standing, or vice versa, with all their levers and tilting action. If you happened to catch all three in recliner mode, your vision was one of soft white flesh spilling over brown leather, bathed in the white phosphorus light of the TV.

I was able to complete my high school requirements by the end of eleventh grade, making it possible for Lisa and me to graduate together in 1975, with the immediate family and various other relatives in attendance. We then headed up to Canada. Since my parents couldn't afford to send us both to college the same year, the plan was that I would stay and do grade thirteen in Canada. At the time, grade thirteen was required in Canada for students planning to transition to a university. Lisa would come home and get ready to head back to university at USC, and I would follow a year later. For both of us girls there was simply no choice in where we went to school. We would go to USC—Lisa this year, me the next—because South Carolina was our last U.S. residence, so we got in-state tuition, and Momma and Daddy knew folks, in case we got into trouble or had a problem.

It is a credit to both of my parents that they never let on what a strain university tuition was for them. Momma said, "Our commitment to you is to cover four years of college tuition, and the first two years of basic room and board. That's it. Anything else you have to earn." For Lisa and me, college and graduation from it in four years was a rock solid expectation. The fact that we had to contribute to our sustenance, and pay for all of our bells and whistles, taught us to regard it as a privilege, make a commitment to perform somewhere close to our potential, and work. The fact that we were so far from our family ensured that sisterly friendship trumped competition. It also taught us to be truly independent.

Before I joined Lisa at USC in 1976, I spent a year in Toronto having a few other transformative experiences. Because I'd been smart enough to graduate at the end of eleventh grade, I was thought of as the intellectual in the family. However, living in Toronto and participating in grade thirteen taught me how to learn, research, and write. It laid the foundation for my intellectual success and for that, I am truly grateful. The downside was that it was lonely. I made no real girl friends. There were only a small number of grade thirteen students, and only two of us were girls. But the truth is, I did not make much effort, since I knew I was leaving in a year for college—again that attitude/expectation issue. I have learned that the universe continually gives reinforcement lessons if I am willing to receive the booster.

That year, I took North American history and, in that it was being taught in a Canadian school, it was taught from a totally British perspective.

The American Revolution was the revolt of the colonies. The Boston Tea Party was simply the wasteful and wonton dumping of tea into the Boston Harbor by rebels. American independence and bravery were colonial ungratefulness and folly. The us versus them attitude was everywhere. In Canada, Pakistani immigrants were talked about and stereotyped in the same way that Blacks and Native Americans were in various regions of the U.S. I learned that nationalism and racial prejudice were not just about language and skin color; economics was also central to these biases. What most groups want is for somebody to be socio-economically below them, grateful for what little they have.

...

Momma had always said that there were three critical agents she made sure that she knew, and that liked her, wherever she lived: the mechanic, the banker, and the pharmacist. This list makes you appreciate her practicality, and her grasp of suburban living. In Toronto, our mechanic became our closest family friend. He was a young Italian man who owned the corner garage and gas station, and went on to be an owner of horses and sports teams. He was a big sports fan and a kind, happy person. He chained smoked, walked with a rocky gate due to his bowed legs, and had brown wavy hair and a ready smile. I'll call him Matt.

I was in love with him, he was captivated by Lisa, and Lisa had no real interest. It was truly a Shakespearian love triangle. It started by all of us going to football games together along with Bob, my boyfriend from Columbia. Then Bob left, and Lisa went off for her freshman year of college. So, Matt and I continued to go to games together and to the receptions they would have after for the team, friends, family, and boosters. The way the triangle worked was that Matt and I would 'date' when Lisa was away, but when Lisa came home he would go out with her. Lisa had no idea what was transpiring when she was gone, and my parents thought Matt and I were just good friends, for that was Matt's truth, and my story.

For years I had had a front row seat to the chemistry between Momma and Daddy. I was also reading *Tropic of Cancer* by Henry Miller for the first time, and was ready to find out what this thing called sexual intercourse was all about. So, one thing lead to another and I ended up willingly losing my virginity to Matt one night after an Argonauts game. The next day I took a long walk by myself along the Mississauga River and thought, "Is that all there is to it?" If I had been more in tune with myself, I might have understood that my feelings for Matt had never been real love or passion, and that competing with Lisa had been a big factor in the attraction.

Needless to say. such a situation will ultimately spontaneously combust. The flames—tears—started when Lisa was coming home for Christmas break. Matt had to put some distance between the two of us if he was going to be able to really pursue Lisa. The conversation outlining this new reality took place in his garage.

Matt was horizontal under a brown car chassis furiously working a wrench. I could see his legs in his grey coveralls and his heavy brown work shoes protruding from the front end of the car.

"Lori, you know I'm really interested in having a serious relationship with Lisa, and she's coming home in two weeks," he said into the body of the car.

I was shocked. I thought we were past all of that since we were now having sex.

"Lori, you're my good friend," Matt continued.

"But we've had sex," I said as I began to cry.

"Friends have sex all the time. It doesn't mean that I'm in love with you. I don't feel the same way around you as I do when I'm with Lisa."

"Why not? What does that feel like? I don't understand. I love you," I sobbed.

It was perfect; he did not have to look me in the eye, and I was free to cry and carry on while sliding around the edges of the garage walls.

Eventually, Matt and I became good friends. We continued to know and see each other in our adulthood, across marriages and children. And, until Lisa read a draft of this book for the first time she never had a full picture of Matt's and my relationship. Once she did, she called me and apologized for how hurtful that must have been for me.

...

In the spring of 1976 I graduated grade thirteen as an Ontario Scholar. This meant that I could attend a Canadian university, if I so desired. I toyed with the idea of going to the University of Toronto, but ultimately, I was a Southern girl, so I joined Lisa at USC.

Like any good Southern girl of that time, I rushed and joined a sorority as fast as I could. This was very important to my mother since she had been a sorority girl, and she felt that being a member of such a group would secure for us girls a gentle bosom of security and support.

For rush week, hundreds of white girls in sundresses and T-strapped sandals or espadrilles, with big hair and full makeup, clutching small cloth or leather purses congregated in the sorority quad. We were then divided into groups, and paraded through one sorority meeting room after another where we met more girls named Mary, and Sky, and Susan than we could possibly remember, and talked about the same things over, and over, and over again. It was speed dating for girls only, and it was painful and cruel if you were not an alpha girl.

I was not, but Lisa was. I had never been good at small talk and petty girl stuff, two elements that were critical to rush week. But Lisa navigated me through it. She took me by the hand, introduced me to her sorority sisters, and helped carry the conversation.

"Sky, I want you to meet my sister Lori. She's just spent a year in Canada completing grade thirteen."

"Grade thirteen? I've never heard of such a thing? What's that like?"

"It was hard, but interesting. I studied American history from the British perspective. To the Brits the American Revolution was a revolt."

"A revolt? My goodness," Sky said, "Can you believe that? Let's just be thankful we won then. Those British might've made slaves out of us."

Sky passed me off to Susan, and the routine began again.

I found the whole experience so painful that when I got back to my dorm that first night I called my mother crying. "Mom, I can't do this. I just hate all the vacuous conversations, the constant judgement of other girls. They're more critical than Daddy could ever be."

"Lori, I get that this is hard for you, but you can do it. I think it's important that you be a member of a group like this since your dad and I are so far away. I want you to have a community. You'll see, your sisters will support you."

While the sorority itself never meant that much to me, it did give me opportunities to be involved and excel. I credit my sorority days with facilitating my membership in Mortar Board and Phi Beta Kappa, among other honorary societies. If you value where you end up, you cannot lament the path that got you there.

...

The summer after my freshman year, Lisa and I both got jobs as cocktail waitresses in Toronto. We could live at home, and save money. There I met Barry, the first man I ever had real, powerful chemistry with. He was a thirty year old British drummer who was the band leader at the bar. He was short and stocky with dirty blonde hair, and a wonderful accent. The bar was a high class saloon, with a live show and band. It had sawdust on the floor, an elevated stage with a three-sided balcony overlooking it, and a series of nightly shows which included singing, dancing, and short skits given by Ms. Kitty. One night Barry stopped me after a particularly painful evening of waiting on a table of rowdy, drunk women celebrating a bachelorette party. I was fried and he could see it, so he invited me out for a drink or breakfast, my choice. We went to an all night diner and talked until five in the morning.

That was the beginning of what I term our seasonal relationship. We saw each other once every season in one city or another across the U.S. for about two years. This was made possible by the fact that Barry had auditioned for Tom Jones and his band and had been officially hired as

Tom's drummer in September, right about the time I headed back to school. The first time I met him on a Tom Tour, we had yet to consummate our relationship. When we did, Barry was such an attentive lover, and lover of women, that he took me to places I had never been before, and rarely since. He also told me that he hoped he knew me over the years because he could see that I was going to be an amazing woman. That guy went a long way in helping me cultivate a sense of my worth, and open up sexually.

On one seasonal adventure, I met him and the band in Las Vegas. Barry picked me up at the airport in a limousine, and off we went to Caesar's Palace. At that time, 1978 or 1979, Las Vegas was simply the strip. It still had a good bit of the wild west feel, accentuated by the fact that it sat in the middle of the desert like the yolk of a fried egg. There simply were no suburbs surrounding the strip at that time, and at night all that neon gave off a warm yellow glow.

On that trip, I got my first close up experience with the western desert. One morning Barry and I set off in a rental car to Lake Meade. We had the windows rolled down, and the road was empty, so we were speeding through the desert with Earth, Wind, and Fire playing on the car cassette. The desert was endless, quiet, and calm. The wind was tangible and rushing. I felt so totally alive that my whole body was humming. As we crested the ridge and the lake spread out before us, I had the feeling of coming upon the promised land. On the way back we stopped at a roadside diner, and Barry taught me to drink coffee while charming me with tales from the road.

It is clear, looking back, that Lisa and I were both working through some Daddy issues. We were both carrying on with older men, which made it quite hard for the boys in our orbit to compete. Apparently, Lisa had a few more daddy issues than I did, because she had a few more older fellows sniffing around her. One was an influential governor of an east coast state, another a head collegiate football coach, and still another a young assistant coach at USC. I can't speak for Lisa, but I can say for myself that I would not trade the older man experience for anything before or since. In fact, on some level it stuck; both of my husbands have been quite a bit older.

In this second year of living in Canada, my parents tried out the local sport of couples curling, thinking it would be a thing that they could do together and a way to meet some folks that were not related to football. After the first thirty minutes, they both knew they would not be returning. Curling involves moving a large granite disc from one spot on a sheet of ice to the target at the far end of the lane. You can think of it as shuffleboard on ice. To propel that granite disc, called the rock, you have to lunge and thrust it across the ice. When it was Lamar's turn at bat, so to speak, he would use his arm strength to motivate the forward movement of the rock, but he had to throw himself down on his side on the ice to get down low enough to be effective.

His old football injuries meant that he simply could not bend his knees and execute anything approaching a squat or lunge. But his competitive nature ensured that he was in it to win it. Apparently, between his concentration and the icy surface, he experienced a potent numbing agent, because my father did not feel a thing while he was playing. Yet, when he woke up the next morning, he was black and blue up and down the right side of his body. He concluded that there was too much pain for so little action. He said, "You know, if I'm going to get banged up like this, I might as well be playing football. At least then I'd have some money to show for the abuse."

...

Over the next few years, Lisa and I both did well in school, worked to support our living expenses, and took road trips to the beach or mountains when the opportunities presented themselves. At this time, I was working two jobs, and cultivating a circle of friends that included a number of artistic types, foreign students, and intellectuals. I was also doing my fair share of drugs, having adopted the Leachman approach of work hard, play hard.

One of my friends was a wealthy young man from Venezuela who went by the name of JC. His family had a home in Hilton Head that became the go-to place for my crowd when nothing would do but a road trip. On most occasions there would be over twenty people staying at his condo at one time. The blender would be working day and night, pot smoke would hang heavy in the air, and people would have fallen where they were standing when they passed out, or simply had to take a rest. From mid-afternoon until the early hours of the morning, some combination of live and recorded music would be playing. Folks would be swaying, pumping, and shaking to the rhythm. It was a wild, convivial affair, and a good way to let off steam and return committed to your academic tasks in the week ahead.

Over the years, Hilton Head held a special place in my heart and my family story. When you hit the bridge that led onto the island, you could always count on experiencing the aha! funky Southern smell of arriving home. On these early excursions, the island was simply a sleepy little spot with starry skies and wide, white sandy beaches. It was not until a few years later, when I was dating a real island boy, that I discovered such secret places as the Golden Rose Cadillac—an authentic after hours juke joint in the backwoods. Now gone. And even years later still, when it became our regular Leachman family vacation spot, I played on those white sandy beaches with my own boys. Now grown.

On another college road trip, three friends and I loaded up my little Chevy Chevette and headed to the west coast of Florida. We were looking for a quiet, cheap place to spend spring break. The first night we ended up in Bradenton Beach, Florida. It was late at night when we finally found a place that had a room and would rent it to us. The four of us peeled ourselves out of the car and settled into our room. Included in the group were two girlfriends of mine, Lisa and Karen, and one of my best guy friends named George. The next morning when we woke up we opened the curtains to find a line of old folks parked in their fold out chairs on the sidewalk across the parking lot from our room. Every single one of them had a laser like focus on our door. When George walked out to get some ice, the men practically fell out of those chairs in their anxiousness to ask how it was that a single guy could end up with three young women.

"Buddy, we hear you got three young women in there with you," yelled the shriveled up dude in the blue baseball cap.

"I sure do," said George puffing his chest out as he strode over to the ice machine.

"How'd you manage that son?"

"I'm doing all the driving," he said with a laugh.

"You drivin' anything else?" the shriveled man asked. The entire group fell out laughing.

Later on we joined some of them at the picnic tables on the premises. We learned that we were staying at a motel/retirement home—we had no idea such combinations existed. They learned that we were all just good friends, with little money, but plenty of time. The residents invited us to the local VFW that evening for a party. However, we choose to go to a biker bar that we had heard about in the area instead. That ended up being a poor choice because, once again, the fact the George was accompanied by three young women drew unwanted attention.

"Lori, do you see the way all the guys in here are looking at me?" George yelled into my ear.

I scanned all the leather in the bar and, sure enough, most of the males were checking out our group, giving George the up and down assessment women usually use on one another.

"I think one of these guys is going to try to fight me."

"Don't be ridiculous, George."

Just as the words left my mouth, a meaty, leather clad man who had to be six and half feet tall bumped right into George in a purposeful way. We had to make a quick, sly exit to avoid a fight.

The year was 1980, and at this time in America across college campuses, sexual mores were in complete flux. Gay and lesbian issues were just beginning to be discussed seriously. Coed dorms were being introduced. The one night stand was not common, but was not shamed or talked about. A girl could ask a boy on a date. A boy could ask a girl to pay. You could have a guy friend, period. It was confusing and liberating.

One day that spring I walked in on my college roommate Anne, in bed with another woman. I had no idea what I was seeing until Anne told me that she was a lesbian, and the other woman was her girlfriend. Eventually, Anne 'married' her long-time girlfriend and I gave her away at the wedding, since neither of her parents chose to attend. Both brides wore white, the chapel was pink, and the music and dancing that followed was kinetic, joyful, and orgasmic. They are still married today.

When Daddy met her for the first time, he said to me, "That girl may not know it, but she's a homo."

"The term for women is lesbian dad, and, she knows who she is," I responded with amazement. I had lived with Anne for more than a year before I found out about her preferences. Even then she had to tell me. My dad could just sense it.

"Lesbian, huh?" He tucked that bit of information into his growing sexual lexicon.

...

During the spring of 1978, Daddy was hired away from the Argonauts. Joe Scannella, who was replacing Marv Levy as the head coach of the Montreal Alouettes, drafted my father into the position of Alouettes' defensive coordinator. Joe was a good coach who knew his football, and the team had a winning tradition. The Argonauts, on the other hand, had continued to struggle. My father did not hesitate to join the Alouette team. Momma packed up again, and she and Lamara headed to Montreal.

Montreal at the time was in the throes of its enchantment with the Quebec separatist movement. The movement called for secession from Canada and formation of an independent, French-speaking country. Momma and Daddy arrived at a moment when Quebec citizens were angry and belligerent. In part, this anger manifested in their refusal to speak anything but French.

Lisa and I headed home that summer to once again wait tables, and save money. Having taken years of French in high school, we volunteered early one summer day to drive into the little town of St. Anne de Bellevue and pick up lunch for Momma, Lamara, the house fix-it crew, and ourselves. We ordered what we wanted and settled in to wait. The waiting grew from ten minutes, to twenty, to thirty. At that point I politely went up to counter to inquire about what was taking so long. A good deal of back and forth transpired until finally an older woman who spoke English was brought out. She proceeded to tell us that it takes time to prepare 200! chicken dinners. Protests all around followed, and we ended up paying for what had been cooked so far. We gathered the food up and headed home, where we ate a good bit of chicken in the days that followed.

Given the separatist furor, you could not get a job unless you were fluent in French—a thing that Lisa and I clearly were not, given our lunch counter encounter. So, my father arranged for us to get jobs waitressing at the Elite English Golf Club. At first we were most thankful for the work. But, as the days went by, we came to loathe that place and that job. You were compensated with a flat fee based on a set number, in theory, of hours per week of work. Since no money ever changed hands in the club—unless it was betting money—there were no tips, and there were even fewer thank you's or excuse me's. It was one of those clubs where the wives and families were allowed in only on certain days of the week, or special occasions, and the upper floors were reserved as sleeping quarters for (male) members who could not make it home because they were inebriated, or separated, or just needed some space.

There was one room in the club, the Buffalo Room, that was permanently off limits to anyone of the female persuasion, except the help. Predictably, the room was decorated in leather, dark wood paneling, and heavy furniture. A great variety of stuffed animal heads from members' big game hunts were mounted high on every wall. Over the massive stone fireplace at the eastern end of the room hung an impressive buffalo head. In theory, it was a big honor to get asked to work the Buffalo Room. That was an honor that was bestowed on me since I had had cocktail waitressing experience, possessed ample bosoms, and had come into my own sense of sexuality, thanks to Barry.

It was in this room that I really learned to hate golf and everything this club stood for. The men were all old—at least to me at the time—white, narcissistic, and totally wrapped up in what they had shot where, and what they were thinking when they did it. They would speak to you about their game like they were whispering the sweetest or cleverest thing you had ever heard in your ear. You, in turn, were expected to react as if that was, in fact, exactly what they had just done.

"Lori, I can't help but notice your name." My name tag was positioned strategically over one breast. "Did you know I played my best game ever today?" The man telling me this was at least sixty years old, with a pot belly. His white, sun-burnt skin was punctuated with burst capillaries across his nose, cheeks, and chin, and his comb over had been dislodged by the wind in such a way that it now sat across the back of his head like a prayer cap.

"I had no idea." I smiled at him beatifically. "That must feel great. What will you have to drink to celebrate?"

"I'll have a gin and tonic. Bombay Sapphire, no lime. I even made a birdie on the tenth hole." He sat up straighter as he said this.

"Well then, why don't you make it a double."

"Excellent suggestion young lady. I can see that you understand what it means when a man achieves a personal best. I bet you have lots of boyfriends." He smiled encouragingly, as if he had just paid me the highest of compliments.

One day, right after my stint in the Buffalo Room, my dad picked me up from work. I had had a particularly bad day that day because it was family day. Family days were always more challenging than when just the men were present, because the wives were bitchy, frustrated, or just plain mean, and, the children were spoiled, and ill-behaved. I had had to wait on them throughout the morning, and then spend the last two hours of my shift in the Buffalo Room. When Daddy asked me about my day, I unloaded.

"I've had the worst day," I said as slid into the car, and tucked myself into the seat beside him.

"Hey, that's a good job with good pay. What could be so hard about waiting tables?" He said as he pulled around the circular driveway and into the street.

"Have you ever done it? Have you ever had to listen to a table full of ten year old kids ordering you around for more coke? Another thing of french fries? A sundae? And then had to clean up their mess when they used those extra fries in a food fight? Have you ever had to listen to old, white, fat men telling you about their golf game, or, how fetching you look in this ugly uniform? If you do the math, my hourly wage comes to almost $2.20 an hour. All the hassle might be worth it if I could count on tips to up my take."

He thought on that and turned to me as we were pulling into our driveway and said, "Well, I hope you're stealing from them then."

At that point I opened up my purse and showed him the multiple place settings of silver plate that I had managed to procure that day. I could tell he was proud as he could be of my resourcefulness. He broke into a big grin and busted out laughing, "That's my girl!" That silverware became our little secret, shared with Lisa, since she was in on the heist from the get-go. It saved Lisa and me the expense of having to buy any kitchen utensils that fall when we moved into our first apartment off campus.

Daddy taught us to root for the underdog and question authority. His attitude came from his belief in the power of the spirit to overcome the limitations of the flesh; from his belief in mind over matter, and the ability of will and purpose to lift a person or team beyond their natural potential. His sense of rebellion came from his wild stallion nature. Our character did not spring from such noble or feral sources.

We all silently acknowledged that if you employ thinking people, they will figure out a way, tangible and/or intangible, to make what they think they are worth, or at least get closer. Since I was a thinking person, was under-compensated, was less noble, and golf and waitressing did not lift me up, I relied on other mechanisms to achieve a living wage.

...

That first year in Montreal, Daddy really got into the Christmas spirit. This might have had something to do with the snow and the scenery, but truly, he had always loved holidays and celebrations. He loved Christmas for all of the lights and pageantry. He loved Halloween for all the costumes and candy. He loved the 4th of July for the fireworks. On Christmas Eve that year we put Lamara, who was seven or eight by this time, to bed early so that Santa would have plenty of opportunity to stop at our house. As soon as she was tucked securely in, my dad found a broom and an old red rain boot. He placed the rain boot over the handle of the broom and got some cotton balls which we all assisted in gluing to the shaft. He then drew a pair of eyes with a black marker on the boot tip and placed a stocking for a cap on the heel. He put on his jacket and boots, and headed outside. We waited inside. Under Lamara's second floor bedroom window, he bounced that red rain boot up and down, and repeatedly yelled, "Ho! Ho! Ho! Merry Christmas."

Lamara came flying out of her room, yelling from the top of the stairs, "It's Santa! He's here! Santa's here! I saw him." Momma told her to get back in bed. Quick! Or Santa might just pass us by. She jumped back in bed and feigned sleep. When Daddy came back inside we reported what had happened. He laughed and laughed, a deep laugh that reached his eyes, and made his crow's feet more noticeable. For the rest of the evening, every so often he would break into a soft little chuckle as he thought about his caper.

That same Christmas, Daddy got all of us 'older girls' neon orange track suits. Lamara was spared due to her size. Nothing would do once we unwrapped them but for mom, Lisa, and me to put them on and wear them all day. "Girls, why don't all of you put your new track suits on and we'll take a family picture?" Daddy said. He was so proud of himself for that purchase; he thought they looked great with our red hair. We knew they looked awful, that they clashed with our hair, because we could differentiate orange from red from maroon. The truth is that no one in their right mind would wear these track suits unless they wanted to be mistaken for the orange cones and barrels you see in construction zones on the freeway. Lisa and I disposed of ours in short order when we got back to school. Mother had to wear hers for years—it probably saved her from being hit by a car a number of times.

That first football season and the next, the Montreal Alouettes earned a trip to the Grey Cup. The Grey Cup is the CFL equivalent of the Super Bowl. It is played on what is typically Thanksgiving weekend in the U.S., but not Canada, since their Thanksgiving is in October. The timing of the game meant that Lisa and I would be home from college on a break, and could be there for the entire spectacle. What I recall of the experience is twofold. First, it was cold and we lost, both years. Second, the crowds were large and rowdy.

In Canada beer drinking was and is an integral part of any sporting event. In the 1970s in Canada it was sold in the stadiums—this is long before such policies were adopted in the U.S. As the games progress the crowds get more and more boisterous and unruly. By the end of a game a crowd could be in a frenzy. And so it was when the Alouettes lost the game and the title. By the time the Grey Cup had been presented, and the fans began to pile out of the stadium, those on our side were in the throes of sports agony. They were moving as one fast paced, surging river for the exits. I got caught up in that river and moved along for a few hundred feet without my feet ever touching the stadium floor. It was terrifying being crushed and transported by the agony of defeat.

However, Daddy's team was a championship contender. So, the NFL gave him a call. The next season he was hired by the New York Giants as defensive line coach.

CHAPTER 11

A Giant Leap

"Things turn up for a man who digs."

American proverb

"Great abilities produce great vices as well as virtues."

Greek proverb

"The obstacle is the path."

Zen proverb

Momma packed bags, and sorted and boxed household items. Mom, dad, and Lamara returned to the United States, settling in Ridgewood, New Jersey. When Daddy was hired by the Giants, he was working under a new head coach by the name of Ray Perkins. Ray stayed with the Giants for two years before he left to assume the position vacated by Bear Bryant at the University of Alabama. Ray was replaced by Bill Parcells.

Parcells is another football legend. He was recently inducted into the Pro Football Hall of Fame. At the time he began as head coach for the Giants he was somewhat insecure. He was nicknamed the Tuna because no matter how much weight he gained or lost, his mid section was always larger than any other part of his body. Bill Belichick was the defensive coordinator. Even in those days, Bill was humorless and stingy with praise. Other members of the staff included Ron Erhardt, Romeo Crennel, and Fred Hoaglin.

The first few years Daddy was with the Giants were a building period. The pressure was relentless, and not all football fans exercised grace or restraint. After one particularly hard fought game against the Philadelphia Eagles in Philadelphia, my dad came home and said it had been the most hostile crowd he had ever been in. When he came off the field he had spit in his hair. At another away game, as the team was returning from the West Coast, the plane had mechanical trouble. The flight was diverted to Washington D.C., due to the better emergency services at Ronald Reagan Airport.

When Daddy did finally make it home he reported, "When the crew came through the cabin to inform the coaching staff of the situation, the team chaplain barfed into his barf bag. Can you believe that?"

"Well what'd you think Daddy?" Lisa asked.

"I knew if we could get on the ground we had a chance. The issue was with the landing gear. So I was afraid, but not panicked."

"Dad, how'd the team react?" Lamara asked.

"Well, the crew asked us coaches to tell them, so each of us took a group and spread the word. They all joked about putting on their jerseys so that the rescue crew could identify the bodies. That chaplain though, he was a big disappointment. Guess he doesn't have any better relationship with God than the rest of us."

By this time it was the 1980s, and my dad was approaching fifty. He had a full, beautiful head of curly silver hair and had maintained his sculpted upper body. To quote Phil Simms, "Lamar had swag, as the players would call it today." He was the embodiment of physicalness and masculinity of a certain sort; he was football personified.

In football, the biggest coward on a football team is still a tough guy. Daddy was tougher than tough, and he communicated this to all of the players. He had a self-deprecating sense of humor which was tinged with astute observations. He was affable, and quick with a comeback. He was not the least bit politically correct or aware, never had been, but few in football at the time were. He was fiercely loyal to the team and his players. He considered them part of his extended family. Just like with us girls, he took great pride in their individual and collective accomplishments, only, he knew how to let them know it. He spoke the language of men in football.

"Hey baby, you sure did look good out there," he would say to one of his linemen as they trotted off of the field.

"Hot Damn boy, did you break the sound barrier? You sure were moving fast," he would tell the running back as he slapped him on the ass.

"Darlin,' you are one tough son of a bitch," he told Phil Simms after he took a particularly hard hit.

In the locker room and weight room he was always joking around and urging the guys on. "Damn boy, we gotta put some muscle on you. You're skinny as a stray dog." Or, "Hey baby, how much you pressin' there? You sure look good." Or, "Darlin' you can lift more than that. I saw the way you picked up that number 25 last week and threw him to the ground. Put that same spirit into it."

When he had criticism or wanted to motivate, he did it in a way that was non-confrontational but effective.

"You know baby, if you don't start doin' better, I'm gonna have to get someone else. Go home and tell your wife I said that. See if she can light your fire."

"Darlin, I know you've got more in you than that. I've seen it. Tap into the bulldog in you."

"Hey baby, on that last play you just rolled over. Are you afraid your panties are showin'?"

"Lawrence, you've got to get-em, get-em, get-em, if you want to make it to the Pro Bowl again. I know you can do better than that."

He just loved the banter, the teasing, the sense that they were all in it together. That only they really knew what the brotherhood of football was about. Only they understood what it was truly like to have your head in the game.

In 1986, the Giants were playing the Minnesota Vikings at Minnesota. As the end of the game approached, the Giants were losing. They had the ball on fourth down and sixteen, and were going for the win. The team was bunched-up on the sidelines, all pressed together to watch the play unfold. Daddy could not see a thing—he climbed up on one of the benches to watch. The Giants made the first down. When they completed that play my dad was so into the game, and so excited, that he stepped forward to run hug the guys coming off the field and stepped right into thin air. Thud! He was face down, spread eagle on the turf.

Phil Simms recalls that all of the guys on the field wondered what was going on, since no one on the sidelines was looking at the guys in the game. They were all clustered around Lamar, helping him up, and dusting him off. The Giants went on to win that game, a big win, making them payoff contenders and eventually, Super Bowl champions, but the only thing the team could talk about on the plane ride home was Daddy, his focus, and his enthusiasm.

...

The Giants were winning, and big times in the Big Apple began to feel like the norm. My parents knew they had finally arrived and were living the dream. My mother was teaching special education, Lamara was in middle school and was old enough to no longer be considered a child, and Daddy was making more money than he could have ever dreamed of as a small boy growing up in Cartersville, Georgia—about $100,000—a pittance by today's standards. In addition, he was coaching some really talented players. In this period, he impressed me as being satisfied and energized; quick with a laugh or a sarcasm. Paula was basking in the glow of the NFL and Lamar, and feeling some freedom from the bonds of motherhood. Lisa married her first husband and was working the switchboard in Orangeburg, South Carolina. I was in graduate school at South Carolina, working on a Ph.D. and trying to figure out what to do with my life.

I was wrapping up the tail end of a passionate two year romance with my old friend JC, and thinking about dropping out of the program at USC. For the last two years I had been moving between time spent with JC in LA, and doing my graduate course work in Columbia, South Carolina. During my California time, JC and I were doing the hippy dippy thing. I was then legitimizing the wild time by working on my Ph.D. in economics. I had developed an interest in economics because I was good at it; I loved the logic of it and the deductive nature of the reasoning, and its graphical framework appealed to my visual nature. When I was offered a generous stipend at the end of my undergraduate years, that sealed the deal.

When in California, JC and I were traveling up and down the west coast camping between JC's gigs in community theatre. When we had to be in LA, we were getting stoned and hearing great music. We had a regular weekly appointment at the Baked Potato, a well known jazz club. We frequented a tight, very red club on Santa Monica Pier where we saw such legends as Stanley Turrentine. We caught Al Jarreau at the Hollywood Bowl, and saw Canned Heat in a funky bar off one highway or another.

With JC, I took my first real excursion outside of North America. Over Christmas break in 1982, we went to Venezuela to visit his family, and check out where and how he grew up. There, the spoken language, as well as the look of the people, was different. More appropriately I should say, I looked and spoke differently. With my red hair and fair complexion, I was obviously not the native.

My red hair had always held a fascination for strangers. When I was a young child living in Savannah, mom, Lisa and I were walking down the street one day when a man stopped, looked at us girls and said, "I'd rather be dead than red on the head." That made me cry, bursting my bubble regarding how cute I looked in my little yellow outfit, and Lisa in her matching blue one.

In Venezuela, the locals often stared, approached, and asked to touch my hair. It was a lesson that I have never forgotten regarding what it feels like to be the physically different one, the minority. I was keenly aware of race, given my Southern upbringing and the nature of the times, but up to this point, I had been sensitized to the issue from a position of privilege and power. In Venezuela the tables were turned; nothing makes you more powerless than the inability to communicate.

In the South, I had grown up seeing poor people scattered like buckshot across the rural landscape. In fact, my dad's family was really poor—something I only fully comprehended when Grandpa Leachman took me on that visit to the holler where much of the Leachman clan still lived. Rural poverty makes a totally different impression on you. It has a totally different feel from dense, urban poverty. Urban poverty assaults your senses. It is in your face, up your nose, and pounding in your ears.

Throughout this time, I was experiencing the call of the wild. I was not fully committed to graduate school, but did not want to work a 9-5 job. Graduate school was a way to be moving forward without committing to change, or work. I decided that was cowardly, so I began interviewing for jobs, and broke the news to my parents.

Every week, from the moment I told my parents in February until the end of the spring term, Daddy would call on Saturday mornings to tell me to stay in school. He would say, "Lori, are you up? Forget about looking for a job. Stay in school."

"You know I can't dad. I need to work to figure out what I really want to do."

"Forget work. You can do that any time. Finish the degree."

"I am not going to finish the Ph.D. right now, but I'll leave with a a master's degree."

"Well then, you'll be nothing but a college dropout."

"Really dad? With a master's?"

These calls came regularly, like clockwork. As the term wound down, I learned to pick up the phone, and promptly hang it up.

In May, I drove into Ridgewood, New Jersey, after midnight, having completed the term, securing my master's degree, and landing a job. I went directly to my parent's room to tell them I was home, and I had a job. My dad sat up in bed and said,

"Forget the job. Stay In school."

I said, "Screw you Dude," and turned on my heels and walked out.

All of the resentment I had felt through the years bubbled up in me and popped right out. Instinctively, I knew that dad's players and teams shared something with him, and got something from him that we, his daughters, did not. I craved admittance to that inner circle; I knew that as a female I would never be allowed access. I resented that immensely, and that resentment simmered in me. I had given him what I considered the equivalent of a playoff berth, and it was not enough. I thought to myself, "What will ever be enough?" From that moment forward, my life became my own.

Momma came flying out of that bedroom like she was riding a broom. "You know your dad didn't mean that. He's happy for you."

"You know he did. He's been callin' weekly, the same message every time. You'd think he'd be pleased that I got a job, seeing as how I'm nothing but a college drop out."

"Lori, you know he admires smarts almost as much as physical prowess. Your academic success matters to him. It's something he can't do, and he knows it." She was the salve that took the blister out of my dad's demanding ways.

...

The job I got, having temporarily abandoned the Ph.D., was teaching at the University of North Carolina at Charlotte (UNCC). During my two year stint there, I discovered that I enjoyed the teaching and the lifestyle professorship provided. So, I headed back to graduate school. About the same time, I met and married my first husband Gerry. He was very talented and artistic, which I assumed also meant soulful. He was older. He had a job. He owned his own home. We had great sex. Given the animal magnetism I had witnessed between Paula and Lamar, it is now easy to see how I assumed great sex translated into a great marriage.

We settled into Gerry's Charlotte home, and I went back to school at USC in Columbia, boarding with a gay couple who were good friends during the week, and commuting back to Charlotte on the weekends. In the fall I got pregnant with my first son Zach. Zachary Chase was born on June 21, 1985. The next week we headed to Hilton Head for our annual Leachman family vacation. As I plopped myself down on a beach towel that first day, my dad said to me, "Lori, you still look pregnant." I promptly got right back up, and headed inside. I did still look about five months pregnant, and I hated that. I was hormonal and sleep deprived, and my dad's comment was a bullet to my fragile heart and ego.

Later that evening, I was sitting in a white vinyl and wooden chair by the bar separating the kitchen from the living area. Zach was crying, the blender was going, people were talking and laughing, and my mother, who was standing over my left shoulder at the bar, was asking me, "What's wrong with Zach? Is he hungry? Is he wet? Is he cold? Do you think he's too warm?" She was cranking up the electric knife to slice the roast, and I was in total sensory overload. I thought to myself, "I am losing my mind in a white vinyl chair." I got up wordlessly, walked upstairs, and started throwing all of our gear in bags. Gerry came up to see what was wrong and I yelled, "We're leaving."

He responded, "Right now?"

"I'll pack. Start loading the car," I barked. We were out of there, baby and all, within an hour.

A couple of months later, needing to blow off steam, I called my mother one afternoon and said to her, "You never told me what having a child was really like." She laughed and replied, "If I had I wouldn't be a grandmother." I was so angry that I hung up on her.

That fall I finished my course work, having, on more than one occasion, taken Zach with me strapped in his carry seat. I wrote my dissertation over the spring term with Zach on one breast, and a pen in the other hand. By the end of 1986, I had earned the Ph.D., the Leachman clan was back in the boy business with Lisa also delivering her first child, a boy, and the Giants were headed to the Super Bowl.

Defeating the Denver Broncos in Super Bowl XXI was the pinnacle of Daddy's coaching career. He and Momma were both just giddy in the period leading up to that week in Pasadena. As a team progresses through the gauntlet of the playoffs, each team member earns the right to buy so many Super Bowl tickets. This is an option you want to execute, since God and everybody else you know wants them. The excess demand and fixed supply of tickets means that you can sell them at a premium, should you choose to do so. Between the revenue from that, and the bonuses the coaches and players rack up with each playoff win, a trip to the Super Bowl is worth serious money. It meant that my family finally moved past the financial hangover from the WFL experience. And, it enabled mom and dad to make some frivolous expenditures.

One night, two weeks before the big game, Daddy came home with a huge wad of bills in his pocket. Momma was upstairs in their bedroom peering into her closet and trying to decide what she was going to wear to what event, and what she needed to pack. Daddy strolled in and tossed that wad of bills into the air and on to the bed, like green confetti. My mother ran and jumped right into it, rolling around like the proverbial pig in shit. To hear them tell it, they carried on like school kids. My mother promptly pocketed a portion of that loot and headed out straight away to buy her first mink coat.

Momma is a lover of cowboy boots, suede, leather, fringe and all things fur. She is not the least bit politically correct on this dimension and she makes no apologies for it. These days, she is known to wear her mink vest to walk the dogs, sporting flannel PJs underneath, and pink Crocs. Not infrequently, her ornamentation will include a couple of pink sponge rollers on the back of her head. You might say this is her more mature version of the chenille bath robe and penny loafers from her Savannah days.

To complement her fashion choices, my mother typically carries a very large purse. When we were young children, exploratory operations in the purse, in search of money or candy, meant that you could lose sight of your entire arm. As we got older, only the hand, forearm, and elbow would disappear. However, as we grew older we became less and less interested in anything that emerged from that purse. This was due to the fact that mother always had loose cigarettes in the bottom of her bag, and tobacco stuck to everything in it. If she offered you a Life Saver from her purse she would pull it out, pick and blow off the tobacco stuck to the sides and stuffed into the center hole, and say, "Here, a little tobacco never hurt anything."

As we girls got older and grew more concerned with the opinion of our peers, she would laughingly threaten to come into wherever we were going in one of her getups. "I think I'll just come in for a minute," she would innocently say as she was dropping you off here or there. Or, "I think I'm gettin' my happy feet," which would mean she was about to pull out her mall dance moves. Or, when car pooling, if she really wanted to make you squirm, "Lori, why don't you offer Sally—or Janie, or Sandy—a Life Saver. They're in my purse."

Paula's fashion sensibilities were also clearly at play where my father was concerned. By the time the Giants were contenders in the Super Bowl, my dad's style had morphed into what I like to call clean cowboy: pressed jeans and nice boots. Years later, I met a woman who told me that mom and dad came to a black-tie New York Giants banquet with dad dressed in blue jeans and boots on his bottom half, a tuxedo shirt and jacket covering his torso, and a bow tie around his neck. She said he was the most striking man in the room, with his halo of sliver hair, his swagger, and his authentic style.

My mother told us later, that on the day she purchased her first mink she came home and put it on. When my father came home she greeted him at the door of their bedroom in that fur and nothing else. The chemistry between them was charged with their desire and humor; they were having so much fun with all of the Super Bowl hoopla.

Lisa and I flew home the week before the game to spend some of this giddy, quality time with Momma and Lamara, and so that we could fly out to Pasadena with the team, staff, and families on the charter. We both left our husbands to mind the boys, get the boys and the baby sitter set up, and meet us three days later in California. The time was one of pure joy and laughter for all of us girls. We tried on our outfits for each other. We practiced our hairdos. We had a home spa day.

Once we arrived in California, the festivities became more varied and organized. There was a trip to Disneyland, a party at Universal Studios, numerous luncheons, and shopping on Rodeo Drive. All of these things were designed to keep the families occupied while the team and staff were secured in a different hotel preparing for game day.

During that week, Daddy had one free night and we had a family plan to spend it on a high-end family dinner. Daddy picked us up in a team car made to accommodate five. We squeezed seven in—mom, dad and Lamara in the front seat, Lisa, me, and our spouses in the back. It was an up-close-and-personal ride that was never-ending. When we had been driving around for over an hour, it finally dawned on a number of us that we were lost. Everyone had an opinion on which way to go.

"I think we were on this street not ten minutes ago," said Lisa.

"I know I saw that sign before," Lamara offered.

"I think if you take a left at the next light you will be heading north," Gerry suggested.

Well, Lamar was wound tight as a tick, and all of this directing and suggesting just flew all over him. When I piped up and said, "We sure are a car full of Indian chiefs," my dad exploded.

"What do you mean by that? Do you want to drive? Do you even know the name of the restaurant we're going to? If you're so smart, where is it?"

I had to be mentally quick to diffuse the situation by saying that we were all leaders, and sometimes that made it hard for any one of us to follow, *or ask for*, directions. Grudging silence fell over the car as we drove on. When we finally did make it to the restaurant, it took a quick, stiff drink to break that tension and help us get our groove back.

Gerry and I were really struggling financially at this time. I had just finished my Ph.D. and was teaching part-time. We had a child, and Gerry was starting his own business. As a result, we made the choice to sell our game tickets and have a nice meal in the hotel with a bottle of champagne, and watch the game on TV. We would then meet up with the family and team at the after party. I lament not being at the game to this day, but I know we made the right choice. That money enabled us to enjoy the trip, pay the babysitter, and pay off some debts.

Daddy was cool with this choice, because he understood what it meant to be financially tight, and how a little bit of money could go a long way in such a situation. In fact, throughout his coaching career his small acts of generiousity with respect to his players and friends provided further evidence of his appreciation for finanacial fragility. For example, in his college coaching days, he had a player who had recently married, and as a result, could not afford food for both himself and his bride. When Daddy found out, he began buying the young man one full meal a day. When the other coaches noticed that the young man was losing weight, they asked him what was going on. He replied, "I don't have enough money to feed both myself and my wife, so Coach Leachman's been buying me one square meal a day." No one else had noticed, and no one else had a clue what Daddy had been doing.

The Giants beat the Broncos in the Rose Bowl that Sunday in what was a wonderful game, if you are a Giants fan. Of course, the after party was a scene. There were a lot of Hollywood types—Tom Cruise, Emilio Estavez, and the like—sports agents, ridiculously rich folks, groupies, and of course, friends and family. My old friend from my Columbia days, Donna Rice, even showed up at that party. This was a real surprise to me. It reflected the fact that at the time Donna was caught up in the celebrity circuit.

Super Bowl XXI was held in late January of 1987. The following spring Donna's flirtations with celebrity and power culminated in the Gary Hart, Monkey Business debacle. Just like in our high school days, Anne, Donna, and I went through the days when Donna was hiding out from the press and the Hart presidential campaign derailed, together. By this time, Anne was married and living on Sullivan's Island, right outside of Charleston, and developing her professional credentials—she would eventually be a regular participant in Fortune's 500 Most Powerful Women's Summit. The day after the news broke, I was heading to Charleston with Zach, to spend some time at the beach with Anne. When I arrived, Anne and I dissected the events and discussed how Donna was changing history. Two days later she called, and I happened to be the one who answered the phone.

"Lori, is that you? What are you doing at Anne's?"

"The semester just ended and I'm here for the week with Zach, enjoying the beach. Where are you? Are you OK? You know you can come here. No one would think to look for you on Sullivan's Island."

She booked a flight and arrived the next day. Zach and I went to the airport to pick her up since, once again, Anne was at work. When she came off that plane I did not even recognize her. She was wearing fake teeth, sunglasses, and had her hair pulled back in a tight ponytail. When we did finally connect, I asked her point blank what was with the getup. She said the press were everywhere. She could not be too careful.

At that point, I told her straight up that that she was being ridiculous: no one would think to look for her in Charleston, South Carolina. That exchange set the tone. In the car on the way back to the island, I mentioned the fact that her actions were changing history. She was clearly pissed off at me. She told me that she did not know that Gary Hart was a married man. Now Donna is a smart girl, so I just could not swallow that line. I responded, "Donna, who runs for president that is not? And, even if that's the truth, for God sake don't say it to anyone else if you want them to think you have a brain in your head." I am not sure we have ever gotten past that exchange. But, in truth, Donna suffered a lot from that indiscretion. She paid the price for the dance in many large and small ways.

From the moment Anne and I had heard the news, we had been discussing the possibilities in terms of outcomes. Being that I am a professor of economics, I bet on financial gain—a book deal, a spread in *Playboy*. But, because Anne is more Southern than I am, she had a bead straight on the center of Donna's heart. She put her money on Jesus. And so it was, in the aftermath, Donna came back to the bosom of the Lord. With the passage of time she also carved out some space in the non-profit world.

Daddy spent a good part of his post-game, Super Bowl evening cranked back in a chair nursing a drink, grinning from ear to ear. He accepted the congratulations and handshakes of all the party-goers with a bit of disbelief. He kept repeating under his breath, "Small town boy makes good. Whew!" My mom was pinned to his side, basking in his pleasure and hers. She was radiant. The rest of us girls were swirling around him like water, then moving off through the room to have our own experiences. I spent a good bit of that evening cruising through the crowd, and eyeballing the people and the scene.

The Super Bowl ring that Lamar received was a source of great pride for him. He did not wear it all the time, since he was not the jewelry-wearing kind of guy. But, you knew if he had it on, he was going out to press the flesh and socialize. The ring is large, size thirteen or fourteen, composed of gold, diamonds, and blue enamel. On the square surface is a stylized version of the Vince Lombardi trophy outlined in blue enamel, and inlaid with twenty-one diamonds. Around the perimeter in gold relief is Giants*World Champions*. On the top left and right corners respectively, is the game score, Giants 39, Broncos 20. On one side of the shank in gold relief is Lamar, on the other, Leachman. Below his name on either side is a Giants helmet. The wives received a pendant mimicking the face of the ring. On the back of each is their name and the game date. Keeping up with Lamar's ring over the years became a big source of frustration for my mother, but wearing the pendant filled her with pride.

After the Super Bowl, my father slipped on that ring one Sunday and he and Momma headed out to 'toot around,' as my parents liked to call it. They started at one of their local hangouts in Ridgewood. As the afternoon progressed, they ended up in one of their favorite sports bars near Giants' stadium. On the way home, mom pulled into the local WaWa convenience store, and dad hopped out. He ran in to buy some more chewing tobacco for himself, and smokes for mom. As he asked for what he wanted, the clerk responded, "Sir, do you regret it?"

My dad replied, "Hell no son. Sometimes you're a winner and you've just got to celebrate it."

The clerk said, "No sir, I said debit or credit."

My dad snapped his card down on the counter and said, "Credit."

The cashier ran his card, and slid his purchases toward him. Dad tucked his credit card into his pocket, palmed the pouch of Redman and mom's Kents, and walked out. As he passed through the door and out into the night air, he chuckled to himself thinking, "I don't regret a thing."

...

The years preceding and following the Super Bowl was a time for me that I have termed the winter of my discontent. There was the stress of finishing graduate school; the stress and frustration of a new baby; postpartum depression; disappointment in my mate; the stress of starting a new business; and financial strain. It was a load to carry, and at a certain point, I decided I had had enough. I dropped that basket and everything in it, except the baby and the degree.

After my divorce, I had my wonderful son, a solid group of friends, and was starting my career as a professor teaching at a small Southern college. I was experiencing my first success with the publication of academic work, and was learning the ins and outs of the academic game. I had grown up with both my father and my mother as my role models, with respect to work. My dad did what he loved, had risen through the ranks due to his talent, drive, and luck, and made a good living. My mother was a teacher, because it enabled her to parent and be present when it mattered most. In part, I had chosen academics because I thought that it was a domain where I could achieve the same things—some success without sacrificing my personal life. Like their work, mine was not a 9-5 job, did not require that one wear a suit, and generally ensured that summers were free.

During this time, both Daddy and I were learning simultaneously that talent and drive were not enough, nor in some cases were they even necessary for success. My mother had always known this, it seems. As a young adult, my mother had told me one day that it was "better to be lucky than smart." I had taken that statement as a personal dig at the time because I was, as I have said, considered the smart one in the family. However, life experience was teaching me that luck and networks were just as important as, maybe even more important than, talent and ambition.

Some time following the Super Bowl, Daddy got an offer for a defensive coordinator position at another professional franchise—good luck? talent? But Bill Parcells refused to release him from his contract and let him go—bad luck? insecurity? Now, the typical convention in the professional coaching world at the time was, if it was a lateral move the team could refuse it, but if it was vertical, which dad's was, they would not. My father was angry and frustrated. But he stayed. A year or two later, the coaching staff was facing some uncertainty regarding whether Parcells was staying or going, and who would follow. So when another opportunity at Detroit presented itself that involved a long term contract and a raise, dad took it.

CHAPTER 12

Motor City

"Don't worry when you stumble. Remember, a worm is the only thing that can't fall down."

American proverb

"A man without guts lives on his knees."

American proverb

Lamar took a position as defensive line coach, with Wayne Fontes and the Detroit Lions, in the spring of 1990. By this time, Lamara was in college, which left Momma to finish out her teaching job alone in New Jersey. As summer approached, mom packed bags, boxed books, and decided which furniture would make this move. The Leachman gear was loaded up, and transported to Motor City.

Mom and dad settled in a house much too big for the two of them in Rochester Hills, Michigan. Daddy simply refused to downsize; he saw the size of the house as a measure of success after growing up in a shotgun house, and sharing a bedroom with all of his siblings. Now, he was also the one driving a Cadillac, which he loved for its floating feel, accommodating interior space, and the cachet of success it gave off. In his retirement years, he drove nothing but Jaguars for the same reasons.

At that time, I was divorced, raising my first son and teaching at a local university. I was dating a younger man, in part, because he was absolutely not marriage potential. Having been married, finished my Ph.D., and now making my own money, I had no interest in being married again. But, I got pregnant, and I knew right away that I was going to have that baby.

I informed my parents at Christmas time, and the campaign began. My mother would not let up on the notion that I should marry the dad, if only for a day. She would pay for the divorce after the baby was born, if I would agree to her plan.

My daddy, however, had a surprisingly different view. He called me one Saturday that spring saying, "Lori, you know your mom and I have talked about your situation. She really wants you to get married."

"You know that's not going to happen Dude. I've been there and done that, and did not find it the least bit satisfying."

"Yeah, I know the time with Gerry was tough, but don't you think it was the combination of the things on your plate?"

"Maybe, but I don't need to be married, and even if I did, this guy would not be the right choice."

"You know Lori, you're a smart girl. You make your own money, own your own home, and are a good mother. I can't imagine wanting to have a child on my own. They're so much work and heartache. But you're a grown woman, and I'm supporting you whatever you choose."

When I hung up the phone, I cried. My father had never said those kinds of things to me in that way. And, I had never fully understood the character of my father, or his common sense and decency, until that moment. Colby Lamar was born on July 5, 1991.

After that, Daddy always joked about Colby's dad's quality of sperm, "That boy must have some strong swimmers. Hope that means the same for Colby Lamar. After all, he's my namesake."

You are probably wondering what it was like to have a child out of wedlock in 1991. It was a relief. It was a relief to deliver a healthy child, especially when you know you are all alone in the parenting journey. It was a relief to not have any expectations of help that would not be forthcoming. It was a relief to know that your counsel was all you had to be concerned with. It was a relief to truly feel the power of your own choice. But, it was also frightening, because this was your basket, you chose it, and you had to carry it all by yourself, no matter how heavy.

...

In dad's first year at Detroit, the Lions did not have a winning season. However, by the next year, they'd won their division and appeared in the playoffs for the first time since 1970. They went on to lose the NFC championship game. Still it was a successful season, especially since the Lions did not have the same winning tradition that characterized the Giants. The consolation prize for almost making it all the way to the Super Bowl for any professional coaching staff is coaching the Pro Bowl in Hawaii. It is a week long party of the highest order. So Momma got a bikini and the Dude a Hawaiian shirt, and off they went with Lamara to the Pro Bowl.

Lamara was able to go along for the ride because that Christmas, while getting her annual exam, the physician detected a hole in her heart. It was a congenital birth defect that explained her inability to crawl as a young child. The condition was quite serious, requiring immediate and major surgery, and necessitating her withdrawal from college for the spring term. Since I had the more flexible job, it was decided that I would come to Detroit to be with Mom and Lamara before, during, and after surgery. Even if he had wanted to, my father would not be present because the team was in the midst of the post-season playoffs, the culmination of the Playing Season.

That's the football life. During the Playing Season, that is all there is. There is no room for anything else, except briefly on Saturday or Sunday night, after you have won or lost the game, and before you are on to the next one. To give an example of just how pervasive this head set was, quite possibly still is, I'll share a story told to me by my mom. When Don Shula was coaching the Dolphins, his wife developed breast cancer. She told various friends that if it killed her, she sure hoped it didn't happen during football season. Don would have to put her body on ice until the season ended. That was the way it was, and if you were going to be a football wife, you had better be hip to the program.

My mother was. So Momma and I shepherded Lamara through her surgery in early January, while Daddy was off playing games. By the time the trip to Hawaii rolled around, everyone was ready for fun, sun, and relaxing.

The next few years in Detroit were a disappointment. The team did marginally well, but it was always a struggle, and winning was nothing you could bank on. During his third year with the Lions, Daddy was hit while standing on the sidelines during a game. He was clipped at the knees, hit his head on the AstroTurf, and was down for the count. His knee was shot, and he suffered a concussion. He carried on until the end of the season, using a golf cart for mobility, and an aide to assist him. After the season ended, he had knee replacement surgery. The surgery was long and complex. It left him with a difficult rehab and a general mental fogginess. He could remember all things football, but he could not recall where he parked his car, or left his keys, or the name of a new player, or how to navigate an unknown stadium.

By the next season, he was still not fully recovered. He pushed through with the aide of Bert, his key assistant, and the handy, dandy golf cart. He also pushed a few of Wayne Fontes' buttons. Wayne had told the staff that they were all free to look for new coaching positions at the end of the season, if they so chose. When one of the coaches secured a job in Atlanta with the Falcons, Wayne refused to release him from his contract. Daddy knew the frustration of that from his experience with Parcells, so he called Wayne out on his pledge. The other coach left, and Daddy was forced into retirement. It was 1995 and my father was 63 years old.

Lamar as he deserves to be remembered

PART IV:

The Off Season, the Recruiting Season, the Season of the Combines

This is the deadest season in football and takes place in the Winter. During this season the team's personnel needs and winning potential are reevaluated. Existing players and coaches are let go. New ones are recruited.

CHAPTER 13

Return Migration

"When the well is dry, you know the worth of water."

American proverb

"Misfortunes always come in by a door that has been left open for them."

Czech proverb

"As distance tests a horse's strength, so does time reveal a man's character."

Chinese proverb

I would like to be able to say that the brotherhood of football that we grew up in extended to the NFL. But that is simply not the case. Maybe it had to do with the really big money that had come to football by that time. Maybe it can also be attributed to the celebrity cult that the media fostered. Ego inflation was pervasive among coaches and players. Everyone attached to the game became a celebrity of sorts, and many lost their way with respect to what was special about football. In some cases, they also lost their way with respect to the issues surrounding what it means to be a quality person. For those who refused to participate under the new rules, or remained naïve in thinking that the game was still central to the enterprise, or that became incapacitated or redundant, the league spit them out.

In theory, the year after Daddy retired he was supposed to be picked up by Atlanta in some coaching capacity, thanks to his Detroit buddy who had taken the job there. He knew he would have difficulty coaching a set position, but he could be a competent strength coach. This extra year in the NFL really mattered to mom and dad, because Daddy needed one more year to fully vest in the NFL retirement system. As he waited around and a job failed to materialize, you could see the disappointment and hurt start to set in. Neither he or my mother could believe that the sport he loved, and the people he liked, helped, and called friends would abandon them. But, with a few exceptions, that is exactly what they did.

I could name names here and list transgressions, but score settling is not what my story is about, so I won't. Instead I want to focus on the measure of a man, his life; how those who loved him lost him; how he lost himself; how we eventually found our way back.

In his last year of coaching, it had been clear that something was amiss. As I said, Lamar could remember all things football, but he forgot simple, non-routine things. This increased my mother's workload in a measurable way, since she was in charge of pretty much everything outside of football and my dad's personal business. Now she had more to do; she had to keep track of Daddy's mind.

By the time they retired and moved to Myrtle Beach, both Momma and Daddy were angry and disappointed. Some of these feelings were directed at each other, but they were mostly directed at all those friends and colleagues who had melted away. Daddy had a number of opportunities to participate in football in productive ways locally, but he put them off. He kept believing that any day one of his buddies would call with a bigger opportunity for him. So he passed on starting a boys camp, working with the local community, giving talks to high school kids, and other things like that.

If he had been more agile at this stage of his life, he might have dedicated himself to golf. But by this time, all the years of playing football in his youth were showing up all over his body. He could not walk well, due to the knee issues and neuropathy in his feet. Back pain was a constant. All the hits he had taken to the head, neck and shoulders, playing center and defensive line, had come home to roost. Eventually, he was diagnosed with neuropathy in his feet, and lower brain stem damage from the pounding. So he stewed.

While my parents were starting their slow descent into an unwelcome retirement, I was starting a new life out west. My boys and I had moved to Flagstaff, Arizona, in the summer of 1993. We had made the move primarily for my eldest son's health, since he was a severe asthmatic, and also because there were just too many men in my life. I wanted to put some distance between my unit and both of the boys' dads. The move worked, providing me with a new sense of freedom and possibilities. Single parenting came somewhat naturally to me, since I had grown up in a household where my mother was a single parent half of the year. Living out west provided me the space and distance to do it without much interference from my boys' dads. Both boys thrived.

We all loved the rugged mountain backdrop and the high desert air. We were learning that the embracing nature of the wind in the west was the sensory equivalent of that aha! Southern smell. We became hikers, exploring the trails in Oak Creek Canyon, Sedona, and Walnut Canyon. Zach's asthma abated. Eventually, we all learned to ski. I settled for my name in print rather than neon, as befits a rock star, and was enjoying the rhythm of the beat of my own drum.

The first full summer that we lived out west, I landed a fellowship at Stanford at The Center for Advanced Study in the Behavioral Sciences— good luck. That fellowship ended up being a turning point in both my professional career and my personal life. I met Peter, the man who would become my second husband, and I made intellectual connections that helped me be a better academic than I ever had any ambitions to be— once again, network effects.

During the Flagstaff years, my relationship with Peter, who was living in North Carolina, was off and on. For much of that time the uncommitted nature of that relationship worked well for me, because I was juggling multiple men, and, I loved where I lived, and what I was doing. I recall vividly a dream I had during this period—I am standing in line at McDonald's, waiting to order breakfast. The line is moving steadily toward the counter and orders are being filled. I am perseverating over whether to order the Egg McMuffin, the Pancake Breakfast, or the Eggs and Bacon Breakfast. My time is running out as the line gets shorter and shorter… It was the perfect metaphor for my romantic situation at the time. Eventually, I chose the Egg McMuffin, so to speak, and he chose me, motivating the return migration of the boys and me to the east coast. The year was 1998.

In these transition years, 1993–1999, as Daddy's mental faculties faded, Momma worked hard to cope and keep the bulk of Daddy's issues from us girls. I was living in the high desert, was coming into my own professionally, and was enjoying every moment of finally getting to live out west. My boys and I would be back east for Christmas and summer vacation, but otherwise it was phone calls and cards. Lisa was living in Myrtle Beach, but was caught up in her own personal hell, which involved having young children, a husband who was addicted to drugs and was mentally punishing, and trying to hold down a demanding job. Lamara had recently moved to the Myrtle Beach area and was starting a new life, with a new job, and a new husband. Within a year, she had a new baby. Within a few years, Lisa was divorced. So we all offered little in the way of help or support to Momma.

It is during this time that Daddy took to the bottle. It began in small ways: with a drink earlier and earlier in the day, a shift to hard liquor as opposed to beer. He became more belligerent and aggressive. This process unfolded over a number of years, so that it is really impossible to pin point exactly when the fun-loving, humor-filled Lamar slipped away. But by 1999, when I married Peter, it was clear that Daddy was no longer himself. He was well into a serious illness that we would not fully comprehend until much later.

...

Throughout this time, my contributions to my parents' lives were unhelpful at best, and completely insensitive at worst. When I visited, I would point out to Daddy what he had forgotten, tell him how much of an additional burden it was placing on my mom, and suggest how he might work to handle the issue himself. For example, one night when I was visiting over the summer, we went out for dinner, then to a bar, to hear music and dance. When we got home that night, my dad realized that he had left his wallet at the bar. As soon as he became aware of the fact that his wallet was missing, he asked my mom to go back and get it. At that point, I stated the obvious.

"Dude, you know that's your wallet and you're the one who left it. You should be the one to go back and get it." Sparks flew between my dad and I.

"Horseshit Lori. It's none of your business." He pressed his face into mine and pinned me with his fierce, focused stare. "Paula, I was sitting at the end of the bar and left it there. Call the bar first and see if the bartender has it."

"I'm doing that right now, Lamar."

I turned to my mother, "Mom, he's the one who lost it. Why can't he do that for himself?"

"Lori," my dad said as he jerked me around by the arm, "why can't you mind your own business? You're just a busy-body."

"What? A busy-body! Because I think those responsible should handle their own shit?"

"All my life I've handled my own shit, and for a good bit of yours, I handled yours too."

And so we went at it, while my mom slipped out of the house to retrieve the wallet.

In the morning, being unable to leave the issue alone, I approached my dad as he was sitting in his large leather chair that sat like a throne in the middle of the living room.

"Daddy, you know I was thinking about the wallet issue as I went to sleep last night."

"I don't want to hear about that again," he said looking up from the sports page.

"Well, I was thinking that since you don't like to use your pockets, even when you have them, you might try getting a fanny pack."

"A what?"

"You know, a fanny pack. Those things that you clip around your hips that have a pouch and a zipper."

"I don't want a God damn fanny pack."

"It just might make it easier for you to keep up with things like your keys and wallet."

His face collapsed, then quickly recomposed itself into a stern expression. Of course this made him mad, and more aware of himself slipping. It breaks my heart to think about how I contributed to his distress, and my mother's, during this time. The only thing I can say in my defense is that I had no real idea what was going on.

As has been established, Lamar had his own sense of style, and it had evolved over the years. The chief criteria for his fashion choices had always been comfort. This made sense: in coaching you have got to be able to move. But, he also had two more things working against him, a complete lack of taste, and his color blindness. During his time coaching in the pros, the team could always tell when he dressed himself and when Paula had a hand in putting his look together. When he boarded a plane for an away game wearing a particularly bad outfit, his players would say, "Lamar, Paula must be out of town. I guess you had to dress yourself today."

In these retirement years, his preferred pants choice was Zuba pants. At the time Daddy wore them, they typically were cut like harem pants, with an elastic waist, some with, and some without side pockets. In either case, Daddy never liked to use the pockets because it ruined his line; he thought his slim, tight hips accentuated his pumped-up upper body. So fashion and vanity conspired: the habit of not using pockets meant he kept losing things.

For as long as I can remember, my father had false teeth—a mouthpiece with a bridge in front, molars on either side. He needed it if he was going to have steak, or something really chewy. He would pinch it with thumb and forefinger, and slip it into his mouth. Since he did not use them all of the time, he was in the habit of losing track of them. There were many occasions when you would find a set of four choppers staring up from the back of the toilet, or the kitchen counter. Restaurant managers frequently called the next day, if my parents had dined out the night before, "Is this Mrs. Leachman? We found a set of teeth at your table last night. Did anyone in your party leave them?" If he did not lose them, he would forget where he put them. Think about that—it is a totally different mental misfire.

On one of the forgetting days, mom and dad were getting ready to go out and needed those teeth. Daddy had no clue where he had put them, and once you had asked, to bring it up again only made matters worse. Momma knew she had to find them herself, since they had a bunch of events that weekend that involved dining. Eventually, she did, and off they went. When they got home, Momma took full possession of the teeth. That evening, after Daddy went to sleep, my mother got the Super Glue and glued those suckers right into his mouth! She figured out that that way she did not have to worry about losing them for the rest of the weekend. She was right. On Monday morning they went to the dentist to explore removal.

The Super Bowl ring was another small item that became a challenge to keep up with. Since it had much more cachet than the teeth, if Daddy left it somewhere, chances are he would never get it back. My father was not much of a jewelry-wearing man, and that was a blessing, as he became more forgetful. It meant that the ring was only worn when my parents were going out together, or there was a large gathering of one sort or another. Mother was the safekeeper of the ring, which put her in a familiar, yet difficult position. They would argue about when, and whether, he could wear it. "That's such horseshit Paula. It's my ring and I want it," he would say. "Lamar, you know you will end up taking it off and leaving it," she would patiently respond. My mother would find that ring in a blue jean pocket, tucked in the tube of his sock, both on and off of his feet, lying in an ashtray, or keeping company with his teeth on the back of the toilet.

...

During the transition years, he also became more honest, less filtered in what he said. He'd always had a way of combining honesty with humor. As his mental capacities began to diminish, his humor sifted away, and his brutal honesty remained. More and more he would comment on the bodies of women and men as they were walking down the beach. He was a man who admired the physical form, and had a clear sense of what he found esthetically appealing. The three key elements he looked for were body definition, strength, and tautness. In our youth his physical fetish had manifested in healthy and not so healthy ways. He was captivated by natural products, and urged them on us. He was also obsessed with weight. If you got the flu and he was checking in, he would ask you,"Have you been on the scale? Have you lost any weight?" Like that was the silver lining to your misery.

His preoccupation with physicality would manifest as unfiltered, crude observations about people he saw, or things going on around him. For example, my second husband Peter is short, solid and not inclined to exercise. As Daddy and I were driving home from the beach one day, Daddy said to me, "You know, I am really proud of you for marrying Peter. He's so smart—the smartest guy I've ever met—except maybe Alton. It's just a shame he has such a bad body."

Such was dad's cutting to the quick of physical matter as he saw it. This comment reflected his awareness of, and respect for, the cerebral as well as the physical. It was also his astute acknowledgement of the nature of my choice.

Daddy continued to drive until a little past seventy. He had left the Cadillacs behind in Detroit and was now driving a handsome, dark green Jaguar sedan. Mechanically it was a challenging car, but Daddy had not purchased it for performance. He brought it for its looks—he knew he looked great climbing in or out of it. He took himself to the gym every day, driving that 'green wave.' If he and Momma were going some place he knew, he might also drive the Jag, as a show of independence and competence, for during this time he could still navigate the paths he was familiar with, but he absolutely could not negotiate anything new or unknown. That meant when Momma and Daddy took trips, they were always to someplace familiar, or someplace where someone else did the driving, like a cruise. The excursions were not memorable for their fun. They served to highlight Daddy's confusion, since anything out of his daily routine could, and usually would, rock his world.

...

Some men are always starched and pressed, some are tucked and trimmed, others are clean as a whistle, and still others have to scrub up before sex and want you to do the same. My father was never any of these. He liked to sweat; he liked the manly feel and smell of it; he thought it sexy on a woman. What this meant for my father was that he almost always smelled like the inside of a medicine cabinet, due to his pill popping. He had been a big vitamin taker for all of his adult life. As I mentioned earlier, he got into the vitamin B shots and other energy enhancers in the 1960s. He was a steady consumer of niacin, E vitamins, and an assortment of other energy boosting capsules. When he was with the Giants he was never without a few Power Packs in his pocket—the pill equivalent of the energy drinks kids drink today.

His came in clear cellophane wrappers with about six or eight different pills inside. An assortment of B vitamins, caffeine, and niacin were included in the mix. They were handed out by the team trainer by the fist full. My dad was a believer in their power and their purity; after all they were natural. If you were not feeling well he would tell you, "Lori, go grab a Power Pack, they're on the kitchen counter." If you had a hangover he would push a Power Pack into your hand and say, "You must have done some sinnin' last night. Here. This'll clear your head," or, "Did you lose your compass? Here, this'll help you find yourself." If you had an upcoming mental or physical challenge he would helpfully offer you a Power Pack or two. "For the road," he would say. My dad was such a vitamin and pill taker through the years, that at the end of his life, when he was no longer really mentally present, he would open his mouth like a baby bird if someone said, "Here Lamar, take your pill."

As Daddy's illness progressed, he continued to go to the gym and lift weights regularly, but he showered less and less frequently. Showering became a big source of friction between he and Momma. Momma said, "Your dad was always good at the smaller elements of personal hygiene, such as shaving and brushing his teeth, thank goodness." But, showering was not on his list of necessary steps to starting a day or heading out of the house. At first Momma could usually reason with him, or bribe him, "I am not going to have sex with you tonight Lamar, if you don't shower." But as time passed, even that did not work. She would have to physically place him in the shower and turn on the water. On more than one occasion the process became violent. When he cracked her rib one day as she was trying to maneuver him into the stall, she knew it was time to hire some help.

...

The driving also became a source of concern. We all were glad that Dad could get himself to and from the gym. It gave my mother a break in her day, and helped my dad maintain his sense of independence. All of that stopped one day when he had a flat tire on the way home. He did not know what to do, nor could he remember his phone number, so he could call home and get help from mom. He just sat out there on the road for hours. It was only Lisa passing him on the side of the road as she was driving to my parents' house that rescued him—a serendipity we were all immensely thankful for. After that, we girls discussed such things as programming the phone and taping a note on his visor outlining how to auto dial. But we doubted it would work, because he had never been comfortable with modern gadgets. So, we rejected all partial solutions and hired a driver.

Daddy did not give up his keys willingly. Momma had to hide them from him and lock the car. She also had to install bolt locks above the doors where he would not think to look for them, so he could not leave the house without someone knowing. This was our adjustment to the fact that Daddy was no longer sleeping through the night most nights. Instead, he would get up and wander, and drink.

My daddy was a charismatic and vital man. He was an optimist and a risk taker by nature. Although he was a country boy, he was smart enough, proud, and, in many ways, very perceptive. Knowing this about your parent and seeing the way he was unraveling in slow motion is heartbreaking, if you have a clear understanding of what is going on. But, as I said, we did not. So instead, us girls were angry and frustrated. When he would ask me for the tenth time, "How much money are you making now? What is it that Peter does? What sport does Colby play?" I would snap back, "I told you dad, he plays soccer."

I suspect my mother had a great deal more sympathy, because I am sure she had a clearer picture of what was happening, although not the why of it. But she was not sharing that with any of us. She was still trying to be the queen of denial, as well as shield us from the worst of it. My dad was 'coping' with his situation by drinking.

The drinking compounded and fueled the anger that was swirling around in us girls. We saw it as a replay of Grandpa Leachman's addiction, and the cause of Daddy's troubles, rather than the symptom that it really was. I can't speak for my sisters, but for me, it made me less generous of spirit, and more righteous in my judgments concerning his escapades.

I realize now that the drinking was my father's way of coping. He knew he was losing mental function and, if he overindulged, he could attribute it to drinking too much yesterday or last night, rather than facing what was actually happening. He could forget, at least for awhile, that he was forgetting. He would do such things as suggest that we watch such and such movie tonight, when we had seen it the night before. When informed of this fact, he would sheepishly say, "Oh right, I forgot. I guess I had too much to drink."

When I would talk to mom on the phone I would ask, "Why do you put up with this? Find a therapist and I'll pay for it. Do you think he's depressed about retiring? This is a well documented phenomenon." She would always reply, "No, I chose him. This is my duty." None of us girls understood this. We constantly discussed that fact that we were in an atypical, highly dysfunctional, frustrating situation, that was as shitty as they come.

And then, one day the shit really hit the fan.

CHAPTER 14

Too Many Hits to the Head

"Troubles are to man what rust is to iron."

Yiddish proverb

"A boat can't always sail with the wind; an army can't always win battles."

Chinese proverb

"You never know how lucky you are until your luck runs out."

American proverb

I t was Christmastime in the year 1999. It was a week in the second half of December. I was done with the term and final exams when Lisa called.

"Lori, mom called. Dad's in Myrtle Beach Hospital."

"What? What happened?"

"I'm not exactly sure, but I'm leaving in an hour and driving down. He's in ICU, in a coma. Mom couldn't really give me any details. The call was rushed, and she seemed a bit unsure herself."

"Okay. I'll be on the road by 2. Should I drive straight to the hospital?"

"Not sure about that. I'll call your cell once I get there, and let you know."

This particular weekend, Daddy had been drinking heavily. The end of football season was approaching. I am sure he was obsessing about who was making it to the playoffs and who wasn't, and the fact that he was not a part of it. Mother had gone to bed early, having had enough of Daddy and his drinking to last a life time. About one o'clock in the morning she was awakened by someone calling her name. My dad had fallen in the kitchen and could not get up. His knee and leg injuries had made it impossible for him to rise from the ground unassisted, since his college days. He was stuck.

He hit the back of his head when he fell. His head came down hard on the metal foot of a bar stool, making a big gash in the back. Momma could not get it to stop bleeding, so she called Lisa and her husband and asked them to drive up and help her get him to the hospital. They loaded Daddy into the car and headed to the hospital on the Grand Strand for the doctors to stitch him up. When they arrived he was belligerent, messy, crude, and angry. He was The Dude, unglued. He was loaded in more ways than one. I was not there, but I have no doubt that he fought with the attendants. So, my dad was strapped to a restraining board horizontally. He was then left unattended. He vomited. He aspirated vomit. By the time Lisa called, he was in a coma in the hospital, in intensive care. He was alive, but barely.

Momma tried to play down the seriousness of the incident. "Well, yes. He's in I.C.U. Well yes, he is in a coma. But I'm sure he'll snap out of it." He did not. He was in I.C.U. for six days, five of them in a coma.

We learned during this time that the only reason he was alive was because his body mass was so muscled, and lung capacity was so strong, that they had sustained him. A weaker man would have died then and there. When we, his daughters, tried to joke with each other about what was happening, we would say, "Well, I guess all that weight liftin' sure paid off."

Suddenly it was clear that things had to change. Yet I was still angry. "How could this have gotten to this point?" I thought. "Why didn't we do a family intervention? How could he have blown over a .3 alcohol blood level and still be alive?" We still did not fully understand what was happening to him or what he was going through, nor what that meant for us.

Over those six days, we scrubbed the house of all alcohol. This turned out to be a much bigger task than anyone anticipated. My father had hidden bottles of various liquors all over the place: in his desk in his study, in a cabinet in the living room, tucked away behind a box in the garage, at the back of his sock drawer in the bedroom, in the cabinet above the washing machine in the laundry area, and even in the back of the bathroom linen closet. We were all astounded by the variety of locations and quantities of alcohol that we discovered.

We also discovered some heartbreaking correspondence he had had with himself. There were notes in his desk in his handwriting, written over, and over, and over again, saying, "Be good to Paula," "Say a nice thing," "Family is everything," and "Man up." I suddenly saw how aware he was of his situation, and how hard he was working to manage it. He was essentially making inspirational notes for himself so that he could overcome his growing losses. And, he was drinking so that he could forget how bad it was. I realized that aspects of his behavior were brave and valiant in the face of unspeakable indignities.

...

When my father came to, he was out of his mind. He knew my mother, but not his present self. In the very beginning, I am not sure if he had any real clarity regarding us girls and who we were. He knew he knew us, but not specifically who we were, or how he knew us. He had no sense of time or place. He would belligerently say, "I'm eighteen. Give me my keys. I'm going out. I have a date." Other times he would be in his early twenties, "Paula, give me my keys. I have a card game with Radar and the gang. I'm gonna be late if I don't get out of here."

The confusion was made worse by the fact that he recovered his physical strength very quickly. He was constantly trying to get out of bed and go somewhere. When he was in the hospital bed and it was cranked back, he could not climb out because of his limited leg action and the torque it took to lift his own weight. But when the hospital staff moved him into a reclining chair, he was off to the races. One day we came in to find him at the nurses counter, angrily arguing for his car keys because he was "over eighteen, had his license, and had a girl to pick up." After that, during his sitting time, he was secured with a straightjacket to the chair.

A straightjacket is one complex affair. The sleeves are over-long, to cover the hands, with straps at the end to secure the arms tightly around the chest. There is typically a strap in the front to further secure the arms across the chest. Down the back are an array of buckles and straps to fasten the garment. And, there are straps that lace through the crotch from front to back, to make sure that it cannot be slipped over the head. Given its heft, it must also be quite hot. To see my father, Daddy, The Dude, secured by the four points, was one of the most humbling and saddest experiences I have ever had.

Daddy did not suffer this indignity quietly or calmly. His brow would be deeply furrowed, his eyes squinted, and his mouth firmly set. He would constantly be arguing with whoever was in the room, and demanding, "Take this thing off." He would emphatically say, "This is horseshit. You know I'm eighteen." Given the story of how Momma and Daddy met, you know eighteen is a critical number for him: he would not date Momma until she 'grew up' and turned eighteen. But until the hospital, none of us girls knew how important it was. Eighteen in America was what he considered a magic number. When he turned eighteen, it set him free to begin his life, when Momma turned it, it set him free to date her. So I guess you could say that the upside of being in his situation was that he was eighteen again.

In the second week of his recovery, I started to notice one thing in particular that let me know he was still in there somewhere. By this time we had established a hospital routine. Momma would go in the mornings and sit with him. She would take *Southern Living, More, New York Magazine,* and others to read. She would get an update from the nurses and doctors regarding his treatment, and sit with him through breakfast. She would make sure he took his pills, and would get him up and dressed for the day. We girls would show up later in shifts. The order of our shifts depended on who had what going on that day.

Since I traveled to the beach from out of town to help, my days in Myrtle Beach were the most flexible. So, my schedule revolved around Lisa's and Lamara's commitments. Some days I would follow Lisa's shift, other days I would follow Lamara, and, on still others, I would be first. No matter the order, when the change-up occurred, Daddy's entire demeanor would change depending on who was coming, and who was going. If Lisa came into the room, Daddy would immediately relax and be pleasant, offering a greeting or a query about what she had going on. If Lamara came into the room, he was non-committal and dismissive. If I came into the room, his body would tense up like he was getting ready to do battle, and he would become argumentative.

He was remembering in large and small ways who we were, and his relationships with each of us. Lisa was the oldest, had always been the beauty queen, and had followed a traditional path. She was the daughter that he got; he understood her best. She had also earned an MBA and was a top dog in a major company. She had always known how to stroke Daddy to get what she wanted; she used finesse rather than confrontation to move his dial. Lamara had always been the baby. But, my father was never a doter, so he had taken her less seriously. She had also achieved less, and was more dependent on my parents. This meant that Daddy still saw her as a child. As for myself, I was the unconventional one, the intellectual, and the one who challenged him. I am ashamed to say, I had also been the one who displayed the least tolerance and understanding regarding his behaviors and what he was going through. His reaction to me was equally confrontational, flip, and angry. He knew who I was! So we fought.

More than once, I was not completely displeased that he was wearing that straightjacket. When I would come in, he would come to attention in his white straightjacket, secured to a blue vinyl lounger. He would engage his legs to pull, and simultaneously throw his upper body against the back of the chair to propel it over to wherever I was standing. The look on his face would be one of fierce determination, mixed with anger.

"Hot damnit. Unfasten me from this chair. Why'd you put me here? I'm going to knock your block off when I get out of this thing."

"You know Daddy, the doctors put you in that because you were scaring the nursing staff."

"That's just horseshit. I don't know the nursing staff. Who's that?"

If he had not been restrained I would have been afraid. That determination though, is exactly what had gotten him out of Cartersville, and into the ranks of professional football. He was a guy that never gave up, and rarely gave in.

As the weeks progressed Daddy grew stronger and more grounded in the present. He was still taking side trips back to his youth in Cartersville, or to early days coaching high school football, or his first college job with the Spiders, but gradually, the reality of room 213 at Grand Strand Regional Hospital sank in. This did not improve his spirits or his temperament. The daily battles, for that is what they were, centered on when he would be able to walk around freely, when he would be going home, when, and if, he could go to the gym again. However, he brought that fierce determination and will to getting out of that straightjacket, out of that chair, and out of the hospital. Four weeks after he was admitted for a gash on the head, he was released, with will intact, but much diminished physically and intellectually.

If you are ever sick and hospitalized in America you had better have an aggressive advocate if you expect to get solid, quality treatment. I became that advocate for the family. I was taking notes, meeting the doctors with Momma, and asking the questions she could not bring her mouth to form. "What is his diagnosis exactly?," "Will he fully recover physically? mentally?," "What are the possible drug treatments for him?," "What did you see on the brain scan?," "How do his lungs look?," "Why is he still not always in the current moment?," "Should we expect a change of personality?," and on they went. While I felt strongly that it was hospital incompetence that had led us to this exact place, we all knew that Daddy shouldered no small part of the blame. That fact alone kept us from pursuing legal action.

When you need quality medical care, it pays to go to the best. This is something we did not do in the beginning, because Grand Strand Hospital had the closest emergency room. We left that hospital with a diagnosis of Alzheimer's Disease. We finally had a name for what was wrong with Daddy. We then went after the best care we could find with respect to brain issues.

CHAPTER 15

The Price for the Life

"I count him braver who has overcome his desires than him who conquers his enemies; for the hardest victory is over self."

Aristotle

"Sometimes people don't want to hear the truth because they don't want their illusions destroyed."

Friedrich Nietzsche

After Daddy's Alzheimer's diagnosis, in the weeks following his release, my second husband and I used our connections at Duke University to get an appointment at the Duke Center for Neurological Disorders. Mom packed Daddy into the car—no small task, given his orneriness and confusion—and drove up to Durham for his first appointment. I went with them the following day. Our doctor would be the head of the clinic, a man named Dr. Schmechel.

During our first meeting, the doctor laid out some good old fashioned common sense instructions: make sure he gets outside in the sunlight for at least three hours a day; create a routine and stick to it; no drinking; no alcohol in the home; no vitamins or other forms of self-medication. His medical team also jettisoned all of his medications in order to clear his system and start over. That period lasted about six weeks. It was really trying, since he was at home, and as his system cleared, he became much more agitated and aggressive. Those two characteristics in a man his size and with his strength—for he was still quite strong and habituated by a lifetime of weightlifting to flex and release—can be problematic for any family, especially one that is all female. So we hired a man to come in and help. He hated that, and let the aide know it. We thought he would welcome the manly presence, since he was totally surrounded by women, but that arrangement came and went quickly in the scheme of things due to my father's efforts to punch the guy out.

Daddy, for the first time in his life, was surrounded by women, and only women. He was no longer in the football world, with all the maleness that entailed, and he could not yet return to the gym. One Friday night I was there for the weekend and all of us girls where hanging out in the kitchen talking about shoes, outfits, and the like. He wandered in in an effort to be sociable, and we never stopped talking. Our conversation was all girl talk, nothing remotely manly. After about ten minutes, dad exploded, "This is horseshit. Y'all don't want to talk about anything I want to talk about." He got up and left the room. Right away, we all felt bad and offered to change the topic.

"Lamar," my mother said, "why don't you come back in here and we'll change the subject. What do you want to talk about?"

"Daddy, come back. We can talk about the Super Bowl," offered Lamara.

"Daddy, want to talk about the new gym they are building on Highway Seventeen?" asked Lisa. "I hear it's a Gold's."

But he was just not up to the task, and we were too insensitive to realize it.

...

After Daddy's six weeks of cleansing were up, we headed back to Duke for a real assessment. That assessment lasted for the better part of the year. It was comprised of out-patient visits and treatments. The diagnosis was bracing, and not optimistic. Dr. Schmechel told mother and I that Daddy had what they would also be calling Alzheimer's. At that point I said, "I have children. Should I be afraid that either of them will get this?" Dr. Schmechel's response was, "No. Absolutely not. It is totally life-style induced. It was triggered by what we call a closed blow to the head." Doctors had used that term before, when he was hit and went down on the sidelines, and, when he hit his head on the foot of the bar stool. So now we thought we knew what he was saying: that the drinking and the two blows that precipitated the two distinct phases of his decline were the cause, and, that he did indeed have Alzheimer's.

It would not be until a few years later that we discovered the actual original sin with respect to the cause of his mental decline. One morning, as I was sitting in my regular coffee spot, reading the *New York Times*, I came across an article about a retired NFL great who suffered from Repeated Head Injury or Chronic Traumatic Encephalopathy (CTE). As I read the article, I realized that everything that he and his family had gone through, the progression of his behavioral changes, the issues with respect to his care, were things that we were experiencing. Immediately, I called my mother and told her to go out and buy the *Times*.

At the next appointment with Dr. Schmechel we brought the article with us.

"Dr. Schmechel, I was reading this article from the *Times*," I said as I laid the newsprint down on his desk. "The conditions described in this article map exactly into everything we have, and currently are, experiencing with Daddy. I am wondering if this could possibly be what he actually has?"

"Ms. Leachman, when I said that his condition was lifestyle induced, football is exactly what I meant. Your dad has had a minimum of ten concussions that we know about. However, it is impossible for me to give a diagnosis of CTE while your dad is living. That's why we're calling it Alzheimer's. To confirm an actual diagnosis of CTE, we'll need to autopsy the brain after your dad's death."

"We will not be doing that," my mother emphatically interjected. "Your dad would not want that."

"Why not mom? It'll contribute to the science, and possibly help others."

"What difference will it make to him, or us, then? He's a good ole Baptist boy and would not want his brain removed."

"Mrs. Leachman, I feel quite confident that CTE is exactly what he has. He also has Parkinson's and lower brain stem damage. These two things are associated with CTE."

"Well then, we don't need the brain dissection, do we?" Paula said, as she pinned me with her stare to make her point. Since it was mother's call, that settled that.

The year was 2005, and we were learning about Daddy's problems at the same time that the rest of America was beginning to hear about Repeated Head Injury, or CTE. In the beginning the media, with ample urging from the NFL, portrayed CTE as just a theory. But then the stories and the evidence began to mount, and in ways that were completely consistent with our experiences.

At the time that my father played football there was no concussion protocol. If a player got hit, knocked out, or was wobbly, he would be given some smelling salts and asked, "How many fingers am I holding up? Can you walk straight? Can you see straight? Do you need a moment to walk it off?" Then he would be sent right back in. My family faced the fact that what had lifted him up, out, and beyond an ordinary life, was killing him. This was the price for his large life.

Lamar Robert Leachman began his football career in a time when the equipment was minimal. He wore a helmet made of leather and had much less padding to the shoulders and neck area. Neck collars simply did not exist, nor mouth guards. There were no compression undergarments or braces. Extra support consisted of taping the ankles, wrists, or thighs with medical tape. You might argue that this was not so problematic since the players were typically smaller, but their bodies took a beating. Today's equipment has progressed in many ways, including harder and better helmets, the introduction of neck collars, the presence of knee and ankle braces, the usage of mouth guards, and more resilient padding. But the size of the average player on the offensive and defensive line, the positions my father played, are now between two hundreds and fifty and three hundred pounds, depending on the exact position. And, the aggressiveness of the play is much more intense.

By the time Daddy's condition was fully clear to us, my younger son was entering middle school. He was quite physically gifted, a strong athlete. He was also mad about football, and begged to play. I could tell he would be very good. At every request Peter and I turned him down, citing all of my dad's injuries and physical issues. When he realized that if he did not play in middle school, he would never be able to play, he cried himself to sleep. I do not regret a thing about that decision, except his sorrow. Nor does he, now that he is an adult.

...

In that first year after Daddy got out of the hospital, with my mother's help, he taught himself to read and write again. Think about what an amazing feat that was, given his condition! In the early days he even worked a bit on math, but that had never been his strong suit, and he simply could not master it. He also returned to the gym and rebuilt some of his physical strength. My father brought his will and determination to healing himself. The guy was never a book lover, and was suffering from dementia and CTE, so accomplishing these milestones was truly amazing. I knew better than ever the measure of this man who was my father, and the devotion of my mother to him and their marriage. I was so proud of him that that year for Christmas, I gave him a book, *Friday Night Lights*.

During this time, he also returned to cigarette smoking. Back in the 1970s, he had given up smoking when he was on one of his purity regimes. In its place he had turned to chewing tobacco once he decided he could take off the hair-shirt and indulge again. He used to say that a small pinch between cheek and gum could give you "a good twirl of the head," and he liked that. But when he came home from the hospital, he came home a smoker. We all assumed that the changes in his brain had caused him to shift back to smoking. We accepted the change without comment. We knew it gave him some measure of comfort. However, it meant that we had to be constantly vigilant, because he would leave lit cigarettes throughout the house.

Since my mom was and is a smoker, adding dad to the mix meant that the air quality in their home went from bad to worse. Every time you entered the place you would confront the smell of stale smoke. Your sense of displacement was heightened by the rather loud volume on the TV, since it seemed to stay on constantly, because by this time Daddy was not a great fan of silence. To up the assault on your senses, was the presence of two small Pugs that would charge the TV cabinet whenever there was a loud crash, gunshot, or explosion from the TV. Since my Dad had always gravitated to the action/adventure genre, this happened quite often. Lamar loved it; it would always make him chuckle and egg the dogs on.

Our family had always been a pet loving family. Over the many years and places we had lived, Momma had raised a variety of dogs. When we were very young, living in Savannah, it was Boxers. It was miniature Poodles by the time we moved to Key West. We stuck with Poodles through all of the Richmond and Atlanta years. By the time we got to Long Island, and throughout our Canadian sojourn, it was Irish Setters. The setters morphed into Pugs in New Jersey. Now the Pugs were charging that cabinet, adding to the the general sense of confused dystopia in the house.

During this period, between dad's admission to Grand Strand Hospital and his placement in an assisted living facility, Peter and my boys came with me just a few times on my regular excursions to the beach. I pushed them, but not hard. The boys were older and had their own interests and commitments going. Peter had a new, demanding administrative job that was all-consuming. I also knew they found the whole scene quite challenging. The smoke and chaos was one thing, but watching my father's decline was worse. It made them feel sad and uncomfortable. On the last trip I made the boys come on—by that time Daddy was institutionalized—they told me that they wished I had never made them visit Daddy when he was like he was now. They said they could not remember who he had been, only what he currently was, and was not.

...

Given the seriousness of his condition, the small victories and progress—relearning to read, relearning to drive, going to the gym, returning to Bible study—could not last. In 2004, we began to look for a place that would take him and in which he would be comfortable. We found a very nice assisted-living center south of Myrtle Beach. I went with my mother to check it out and talk to the management. They were reluctant, given his diagnosis and his strength, to take him. Yet they said yes. Two or three weeks later we checked him in for a trial stay, with high hopes, for Momma was in desperate need of a break by then. It only took three days for the management to hit the eject button. He would not stay in his room. He would wander. He did not know where he was. When the nurses tried to get him in the shower or return him to his room, he would become belligerent and threatening. So he came home from 'camp' early.

Thus began a process of research, phone calls, and visits to find a place that would take him, care for him, and in which he would be comfortable. Less than two years later, we checked Daddy into The Manor Assisted Living Center, with great relief, and went back to our lives. My mother, on the other hand, made The Manor and his care her full-time job. She went every day to sit with him and feed him lunch. She took Lamara's girls by to say hello. She brought the Pugs by to cheer him up. She made sure he had flowers and pictures in his room. She made sure he did not lose his teeth, and that they were brushed. She managed his bath schedule, and his doctor and hospice visits. She did some combination of these things daily for almost seven years. When we girls would ask her why she didn't take a break, take more time to herself, she would respond, "I chose him. It's my duty, and the commitment I made when I made that choice." We still did not completely understand this.

The one thing Momma did solely for herself in this period was take up horseback riding. She had always wanted to do it. She was well into her 'sevens,' as she would say, when she committed to the venture and bought a horse for herself. It brought her a lot of pleasure, until she got thrown form that horse, broke her pelvis, and ended up back at Grand Strand with a room of her own. To literally add insult to injury, Momma had to do rehab in The Manor, around the corner and down the hall from 'The Coach,' as the staff called Lamar. When she found out that she would be going to The Manor as a patient, she cried. At the time it seemed almost too much to bear. But the staff loved her, for she had always been cheerful and quick with a smile, and she recovered quickly. To her great credit, she got back on that horse and is still riding today.

Momma taught me a number of things during this period. The most important was how to show up and be present when you absolutely did not want to be there. She went every day to The Manor, rain or shine, sickness or health. More than that, she showed through her own behavior how to be pleasant and kind when all you want to do is scream from the disappointment and frustration of it all.

Once when we went to visit dad, he had a black eye. "How did this happen?" mom calmly asked the nurse.

"I have no idea Mrs. Leachman, I just started my shift."

"Janice, I know this isn't your fault. I am simply trying to find out if there is some way Lamar might have hurt himself." She was masterful in deflecting blame in order to try to peel back the truth.

I can admit now that I have mastered her first lesson, but continue to struggle mightily with the second.

When my father entered The Manor in the spring of 2006, the physicians projected that he had less than a year to live. Therefore, in short order, he qualified for Hospice Care. By the time Daddy died, over six years later, he was the longest living patient on Hospice Care in the history of Horry County. Now, that is a record you do not want to hold.

And, I can tell you that it was not pretty, or warm, or joyful. But there were some loving and laughable moments along the way.

Once, I brought my boys down for a visit to mom's and we stopped in to see Lamar. My dad was sitting in his wheelchair in the lounge when we arrived. As I walked in and up to him he said, "Ooooh, don't you look good. Want to have sex?" Thank goodness the boys missed it, but I laughed until I cried. I was sure he thought that I was my mom. I told mother when I got home, and we had another good laugh about it. You see, we knew that it meant that there was still a wee bit of his essential self in there.

That essential self that was Lamar was totally bound up in football. We had always known this about my father, but the point was confirmed by the fact that he continued, for a time, to call and run plays. "Three-four defense. Mike stays home." Or, "Slant right Romeo, slant right." He would also recognize, in the sense that he knew that he knew them, his former players who stopped by for a visit. But, by the end of 2011, he was once again making imaginary side trips to Cartersville, enjoying visitations from his dead brothers Charles and Billy, and slowly, slowly losing interest in everything he saw around him.

By the spring of 2012, he no longer could identify us girls individually by name, nor did he speak much. By the fall, he no longer showed any flicker of recognition for us. We knew the lights were going out. His recognition of, and reactions to, Momma went last. He then lost the ability to say anything other than "get'em, get'em, get'em." That had been his standard practice field cry, and it stayed with him the longest. Then, he lost interest in food. Even saying, "Here Lamar, take your pill," would not get him to open his mouth.

CHAPTER 16

The King of Halloween

"Life is a grindstone. Whether it grinds you down or polishes you up depends on what you are made of."

American proverb

"After the rain the earth hardens."

Japanese proverb

"In the end, it is not the years in your life that counts. It's the life in your years."

Abraham Lincoln

L amar's approach to death was no different from his approach to life. He did not give in easily. As mid-September of 2012 rolled around, we all knew he was fading. He had just passed his eightieth birthday. He no longer ate much, although you could get him to drink from a straw. So we loaded him up with fortified shakes and chocolate milk, but for a man his size, they were not sustaining. We could see him shrinking with each passing week. Lisa, who had moved to Charlotte and remarried by this time, and I had been commuting down to the beach about every four weeks, on alternating weekends, so that someone besides

Lamara was there to spell Momma. On my visit in September, I went with the expectation it would be my last. Daddy hung on through October.

On Wednesday evening, October 24, the call came from mother. She said simply, "I think this is it. I'm not sure. You know I've thought we were close before. But you might want to come." From February to June of the past year, I had had a commitment to teach in Venice, Italy. The week before I left, mother called in a panic, because she was sure it was the end. I had frantically pulled together the rest of my stuff for the five months I would be in Europe, as well as my funeral attire to take to the beach. I jumped in the car and drove down. On the way, I composed a large part of my eulogy. I knew that neither of my sisters would be able to stand in front of the room and offer a coherent remembrance, and given that I was quite used to lecturing and delivering papers to an audience, I was the natural choice for the family eulogist. When I arrived, it was clear that dad was in a bad way, but death was not imminent. My mother was just panicking because I was leaving the country for an extended period. She was testing my commitment to be present when the end did arrive. At any rate, it gave me the opportunity to plan most of what I was going to say, and to leave my funeral attire and things I would need for that time, in a bag, at mom's.

So, I had a bag packed at my parent's house when that October call came. I was in the middle of a semester, so I went into work the next day, gave my lectures, and prepared for that show to go on without me. On Friday morning, I drove to Myrtle Beach and straight to the Manor. Momma and Lamara were already at his bedside. His breathing was labored, his skin was translucent, his eyes were shut. Mother was sitting on the bed stoking his hair. Once I took the entire situation on board, I called Lisa and told her to get here, quick. She arrived later that afternoon.

All day that Friday, Daddy hung on. His breathing continued to be labored but steady, the air rattled around in his chest. His eyes remained closed, one fist clenched, the other relaxed. He was curled up a bit on his right side. I took pictures of those hands, for I am also a painter, and had a plan to paint them. I cut a lock of his hair with the intent of working it into the paintings. You see, Daddy had always had a great head of hair, and he was more than a bit vain about it. By eight o'clock that night, the staff sent us home, with a promise to call if his condition changed.

The next morning all of us got up slowly, trying to prolong the morning. About ten a.m. we got a call from Lamara, who had just arrived at the Manor, "Lori, is mom there? Are y'all up? I'm at the Manor and I think y'all need to come now. Hurry!" I jumped in my car and headed down the strip. Lisa waited behind to collect mother, because she was out picking up a few snacks, being ever the hostess with the mostest. By eleven o'clock in the morning, we were all assembled. At some point, we were joined by his long-time caregiver Greg, a very large, very kind, middle-aged black man. Throughout the day, the nursing staff popped in and out, administering doses of morphine and checking on The Coach.

His breathing became more labored, but it remained rhythmic until about one o'clock. Another hour passed; it became shallow and intermittent. All of us, including the staff, were sure he would pass any moment now. Another hour went by.

At that point, I asked the nurse, "Do you think we can boost up his power pack?"

"His what?"

"His power pack, the morphine." Mom, Lisa, Lamara, and I had a good laugh, while the nurse looked on quizzically. "He always took these vitamin packs called Power Packs, " I explained.

"I'll have to check with the doctor on that." She left to do so.

We laughingly discussed the fact that Daddy's will and determination had not left him. Maybe he was holding out for the game on Sunday. At this point, my mother was sweetly holding him, stroking and cradling his head. I held one of his hands.

The nurse returned with a booster and our vigil continued. By this time his breath was quite shallow, and for what seemed like long stretches at a time, his breathing would just stop, only to start up again, right at the point where we would be ready to call it the end of the day. Lamara broke down over this, and left to go home to her girls. About twenty minutes later, dad got another booster, and Lisa and mom went outside to have a smoke.

I remained on the edge of the bed holding his hand telling him it was time to go. Greg was sitting by his side. I reached up to massage his head and kiss his cheek. It was at that precise instant that I smelled that sweet smell of death. Immediately, I knew it for what it was. For those of you who have never smelled it, it is a cloyingly sweet smell. I found it strangely refreshing, like a Peppermint Pattie. As my mother walked back into the room, he took his last breath. I turned and said to her, "I think this is it." I was slipping my hand out of his and she was slipping hers in. And so, he passed a little after four p.m. on Saturday October 27, 2012, surrounded by love.

Greg reached over and cracked a window, so his spirit would be free to go. Mother sat with him waiting for the doctors and the mortuary team to arrive. When they did, Lisa and I headed home, while Paula left with Lamar on his last journey. Being ever his best advocate, she wanted to make sure they treated him with respect, and presented him in what she felt was exactly the right manner. They did.

...

When we got back to the house we popped open a bottle of champagne, drank a toast to his life, and began the communication relay. Some time later Momma came in, and we all cried and laughed over the life Daddy had lived. We had a discussion, that evening and into the next day, about the funeral. The specifics of the funeral service were already nailed down, since mom had had a long time to think about that, and plan it. But we had to decide when to hold it. Since Daddy had died late in the day Saturday, it was not certain that his body would ready by Monday for the visitation. If not, the visitation would have to be Tuesday, and the funeral would be on Wednesday, which was Halloween.

"Girls, do you think it's inappropriate to hold the funeral service on Halloween?"

"Halloween is the celebration of the day of the dead," Lamara said.

"Halloween is just like any other day, only you have an excuse to dress up and carry on," Lisa added.

"Daddy loved a getup, a party, and candy," I offered as I poured myself another glass of champagne. "I think it is totally fitting if the funeral service falls on Wednesday."

We all decided that we did not see any problem here.

The folks at the funeral home knew Momma and Daddy, and out of respect for them both, came in on Sunday to fix dad up. This is what you get in the South, if you are on the inside of the circle; folks go out of their way, offering you small graces, to let you know that you mean something to them. So, on Monday morning, all of us girls met at the funeral home to say goodbye, and slip a little memento into the casket.

We were all surprised by how good Daddy looked. His mouth was shut, so you had no idea he was missing most of his teeth. His hair was washed and styled, so that it appeared to exhibit some of its former thickness. He was wearing one of his favorite sweaters, and a pair of Zuba pants. His long, now thin, fingers were clasped softly over his stomach. We tucked a family photograph under his hands, placed our individual tokens by his side, and had the attendant close the lid.

Over Sunday and Monday, our children and spouses arrived. Hurricane Sandy was barreling up the east coast, making travel a challenge, but everyone had been on standby for a couple of days at that point, so the reserves flew in. The kids provided a distraction from the focus on death. They helped me reorient my attention to the future.

We held the visitation on Monday evening. It was amazing what my mother had done to the reception space. She had pictures, footballs, plaques of one sort and another, awards my father had earned, newspaper articles, and letters and notes scattered, or strategically placed, on every flat surface in the room. Combined with the flowers and wreaths, it was a fine tribute to his life.

There were many things in that room that evening that I had never seen before. There was a handwritten note from Wellington Mara, the owner of the Giants, until his death in 2005, asking Daddy why he was leaving the Giants, and telling Lamar how much he respected him. There was the newspaper article from the *Times*, where they wrote about Lamar's love and use of the inspirational quote. There were game balls from days past. There were wreaths and flowers from various CFL and NFL franchises and coaches. There were pictures of all of us with, and without him.

Just like me, my children and nieces and nephew had never seen many of these things. They cruised the room lingering over a picture, a game ball, a note. At one point in the evening, my older son told me, "I had no idea about PawPaw's history, his accomplishments." I responded, "I have never seen most of this stuff myself, or if I did, I forgot."

Towards the end of the evening, I was sitting on the couch looking through the array of paraphernalia that was scattered on the coffee table. I came across a picture of my dad from his high school days. In it he is sitting on a bench, wearing a crown and a cape. He is accompanied by a young woman sitting next to him, with her own crown and cape. He is impossibly young, expectant, and fresh-faced. I took that picture up to my mother and asked her what it was. Mother said, "Oh, that's a picture of your dad from Cartersville High. He was in eleventh grade, and was the King of Halloween."

When I went home that night, I headed straight for the Halloween candy and made little bags from it. After the service the next day, we passed those out to everyone in attendance, and had them throw candy into the grave as the first shovels of dirt were hitting the casket.

The service was a moving affair. For my eulogy, I spoke about dad's humor, his love of a practical joke. About his belief in the power of the spirit and mental focus to lift a person up, to enable them to go beyond their potential. I recounted his love of football, his role as a mentor of young men, and his life-long friendship with Bud Carson. I ended with a quote.

"Rest is sweet when one has earned it."

American proverb

As the funeral ended, Willie Nelson's version of *Georgia on My Mind* serenaded the recessional.

A well done funeral is a thing to be proud of. Daddy's was; we got notes and emails from folks for weeks after, telling us that it was the best funeral they had ever been to. The best funerals, as well as loving deaths, are celebrations of a life, and a gift of remembrance to the family. If the funeral is top notch, it will lead everyone present back to the essence of the person. It becomes a bridge, enabling the family and loved ones to cross from the process leading to, and the reality of, death, back to the vitality and true substance of the person's life. Lamar Robert Leachman's funeral was just that. The funeral gave us a jump start on recalling the richness of his life. For our children, spouses, and Daddy's caregivers, the funeral provided new information regarding who he had really been, and the life he had led.

All of us girls, as well as our children, had lost sight of the real Lamar. We had been so caught up in the reality of the now, that we totally lost all of the then and there. Daddy's death and funeral released us from the now, freeing all of us to remember him as he was, and as he deserves to be remembered.

That night after the funeral, and after Lamara had left with her girls to go home, Lisa and I sat on the couch at my parents' house and reminisced about Lamar and Paula, their life together, and our childhood. At one point Lisa asked, "Do you remember going to the park with Bud? He was our big brother. I thought having a big brother was so cool." At first, I had no idea what she was talking about. Then she said, "He used to take us to the park, and push us very fast on the merry-go-round." As soon as she said the merry-go-round, I had a picture of it, and him. I felt myself sitting on the floor of the merry-go-round, gripping the bars, as the centrifugal force pulled me toward the edges of the disc. I immediately understood why I had always loved that one ride in particular.

She also told me the story of mom taking us to our first football game. I was three and Lisa four. My dad was coaching high school ball. Lisa said Momma dressed us up one Friday night, saying, "Girls, I think it's time you knew something about football, since that's what your father does for a living. So we're going to the game tonight, and I'm going to teach you." As soon as Lisa said it, I knew it to be true. I had a picture of the cheerleaders waving and shaking their pompoms, and the lighted field. I saw my mother's animated face intensely focused on the game. In that instant, for the first time, I understood that my mother's love of football was equal to my dad's. It derived from her deep and abiding love for him. Her disappointment and hurt about the end days of his career cut just as deep. Their reality must have been twice as hard for her, because she knew that football was what led to his last twenty years of incapacitation, a quarter of his life and hers. It must have broken her heart.

Later that evening, my mother got up and joined us in our reminiscing. She filled us in on some of the details of our life with Bud; about how broke they were, how much he ate, and the fact that his parents never sent them any money. She told us some of the story of her time in the orphanage and foster homes. She illuminated the role of the Tennessee network of aunts and uncles. She spoke about our first football lesson; about the excitement when the offer came to play for the Jets; about the financial strain of the WFL experience; about how and why Daddy left the Giants; about what happened between Daddy and Wayne in Detroit; about the fundamental decency of character that had been behind all of his choices. And, she told us about how they met and the nature of their courtship; the fact that **she chose him**; that she knew instantly he was her guy, and she made it happen.

In that moment she taught me what it really means to make a choice and a commitment, and live by it—what it means to carry your own basket, as we say in the South, without ever dropping it.

I realized that all of my life I had been fighting my dad's influence and will. I had been judging him harshly, without full information. But he had been teaching me how to live life fully, and move through it with integrity. And Momma had been teaching me how to love him.

Miss Firecracker Queen

S ometimes, life is totally unfair. Just when you put down a heavy basket life forces you to pick another one up. The year before my father died, Lamara's husband of thirteen years was deported. Unbeknownst to us, he was an illegal immigrant. An immediate deportation order for him had been in effect for at least fifteen years, and it was finally executed. The result was that Lamara was single parenting two young girls.

Given mother's history and nature, it will not be surprising to learn that she stepped into the void left by Hugo's departure. She assumed the role many grandparents find themselves in today, that of assisting in raising their grandchildren. Instead of shuttling dad around town, she is now shuttling granddaughters to soccer practice, or to the movies. Instead of cooking for my dad, she is now cooking in order to send extra food home with Lamara, so as to lighten her load. Instead of monitoring or visiting my dad in the evenings, she is babysitting young girls, or having them spend the night at her house, so Lamara can have some time to herself. Her commitment to family—above all else—continues to determine the direction and pace of her life.

She does this with patience and love, for she knows that raising children is infinitely more promising than watching capacity diminish, and death approach. She continues to ride and find comfort and joy in mucking a stall, and grooming a horse. She continues to watch and follow football. She celebrates the Super Bowl. She shares these pleasures with her granddaughters and grandsons.

With her daughters she shares cocktails, and laughter, and love.

ABOUT THE AUTHOR

Lori Leachman is a professor of economics at Duke University. She has been teaching economics at the university level for over thirty-five years. She earned her Ph.D. in economics in 1987, from the University of South Carolina. Before turning to literature, Dr. Leachman wrote for and published in a variety of academic Journals. She has been in Who's Who's Among America's Teachers, won the 1995 Student's Award for Teaching Excellence at Northern Arizona University's College of Business, and won the Howard D. Johnson Distinguished Teaching Award in 2002/3 at Duke University. In 1994 she was a summer fellow at the Center for Advanced Study in Behavioral Sciences in Palo Alto, California.

At the age of fifty, Dr. Leachman realized that her life was passing and there were a number of things outside of academics that she wanted to pursue. She took a semester off, and enrolled in a painting course at a local university. That course started her on her second path of professional development, as an artist. Since that time, she has exhibited and sold her art work in a number of galleries and public venues in the Durham area. You can view her art on Facebook or at www.lorileachman.net.

Dr. Leachman never had an aspiration to write creatively. However, in 2012 when her father died, she knew she had a story that deserved to be told. She shared that story with a number of writer friends, trying to pique their interest. They all told her that it was her story, and she needed to be the one to write it. Over the course of the next few years, Ms. Leachman let the story gestate. In 2015, while on vacation in France, she began writing vignettes. Within a few months she had an outline of the story. Over the next two years the story presented here emerged.

Lori Leachman lives and teaches in Durham, North Carolina for half of the year. The other half of the year she lives in Sedona, Arizona where she writes and paints, and is close to her two grown sons who live on the West Coast.

CTE RELATED RESOURCES

Leading CTE Blogs
1. Brainline.org. http://www.brainline.org/com
2. NIH Director's Blog. https://directorsblog.nih.gov/tag/chronic-traumatic-encephalopathy
3. The Concussion Blog. https://theconcussionblog.com.

CTE Research: Foundations, Centers and Articles
1. The Legacy Foundation. http://concussionfoundation.org.
2. The Brain Injury Research Institute. http://www.protectthebrain.org/.
3. Boston University CTE Center. http://www.bu.edu/cte/about/.
4. Matthew Gfeller Sport-Related Traumatic Brain Injury Center at UNC Chapel Hill. http://tbicenter.unc.edu.
5. Plasticity Brain Centers. https://www.plasticitybraincenters.com/.
6. Banner Alzheimer's Group and Mayo Clinic Arizona. https://www.bannerhealth.com/About+Us/News+Center/Press+Releases/
7. Banner+Alzheimers+Institute+and+Mayo+Clinic+Arizona+to+participate+in+multi+center+study+of+Chronic.htm.
8. Cleveland Clinic. http://knpr.org/knpr/2015-12/cleveland-clinic-lou-ruvo-center-brain-health-study-cte.
9. The Mayo Clinic. http://www.mayoclinic.org/diseases-conditions/chronic-traumatic-encephalopathy/care-at-mayo-clinic/research/con-20113581.
10. Balance Assessment in the Management of Sport-Related Concussion. Kevin M. Guskiewicz. *Clincis in Sports Medicine.*

http://www.sciencedirect.com/science/article/pii/S02785 919100007859.

11. Repetitive Brain Injury and CTE. Amanda Perkins. *Nursing Made Incredibly Easy.* http://www.nursingcenter. com/cearticle?an=00152258-201605000-00007&Journal_ ID=417221&Issue_ID=3420523.

12. Neuroimaging assessment of early and late neurobiological sequelae of traumatic brain injury: implications for CTE. Mark Sundman. *Frontiers in Neuroscience.* http://journal.frontiersin. org/article/10.3389/fnins.2015.00334/full.

13. Case Report of 25 Year Old Highlights Difficulty of Diagnosing CTE. Dan Hurley. *Neurology Today.* https://www.researchgate. net/publication/293192157_Case_Report_of_25-Year-Old_ Highlights_Difficulty_of_Diagnosing_CTE.

14. Alteration of Default Mode Network in High School Football Athletes Due to Repetitive Subconcussive Mild Traumatic Brain Injury: A Resting-State Functional Magnetic Resonance Imaging Study. Kausar Abbas, et al. *Brain Connectivity.* https:// www.researchgate.net/publication/266027372_Alteration_of_ Default_Mode_Network_in_High_School_Football_Athletes_ Due_to_Repetitive_Sub-concussive_mTBI_-_A_resting_ state_fMRI_study.

15. Chronic Traumatic Encephalopathy in Athletes: Progressive Tauopathy After Repetitive Head Injury. Ann C. McKee, et. al. *Journal of Neuropathology & Experimental Neurology.* http:// www.bu.edu/alzresearch/files/pdf/JNEN-McKeeetal20092.pdf.

16. Chronic traumatic encephalopathy: a spectrum of neuropathological changes following repetitive brain trauma in athletes and military personnel. Thor Stein, et al. *Alzheimer's Research and Therapy.* http://alzres.biomedcentral.com/articles/10.1186/alzrt234.

17. Changes in the neurochemistry of athletes with repetitive brain trauma: preliminary results using localized correlated spectroscopy. Alexander Lin, et al. *Alzheimer's Research and Therapy.* https://

www.researchgate.net/publication/272408392 Changes in the neurochemistry of athletes with repetitive brain trauma Preliminary results using localized correlated spectroscopy.

18. Role of Subconcussion in Repetitive Mild Traumatic Brain Injury: A review. Julian Bailes, et al. *Journal of Neurosurgery.* http://thejns.org/doi/10.3171/2013.7.JNS121822.

19. Long-term Consequences of Repetitive Brain Trauma: Chronic Traumatic Encephalopathy by Robert Stern, et al. *PM&R Journal.* http://www.sciencedirect.com/science/article/pii/S1934148211005296.

20. Chronic Traumatic Encephalopathy: A Potential Late Effect of Sport-Related Concussive and Subconcussive Head Trauma. Brandon Gavett, et al. *Clinics in Sports Medicine.* http://www.sportsmed.theclinics.com/article/S0278-5919(10)00086-4/fulltext.

21. Long-term Neurocognitive Dysfunction in Sports: What is the Evidence? Gary Solomon, et. al. *Clinics in Sports Medicine.* http://www.sportsmed.theclinics.com/article/S0278-5919(10)00076-1/fulltext.

22. The Concussion Diaries: One Football Player's Secret Struggle with CTE. Reid Forgrave. *GQ Magazine.* http://www.gq.com/story/the-concussion-diaries-high-school-football-cte.

Morgan James
Speakers Group

www.TheMorganJamesSpeakersGroup.com

We connect Morgan James published authors with live and online events and audiences who will benefit from their expertise.

 Morgan James makes all of our titles available
through the Library for All Charity Organization.

www.LibraryForAll.org

CPSIA information can be obtained
at www.ICGtesting.com
Printed in the USA
LVOW03s1347040418
572267LV00004B/4/P

9 781614 488255